THE CREMALDI COOKBOOK

Doubleday

NEW YORK LONDON TORONTO SYDNEY AUCKLAND

THE
CREMALDI COOKBOOK

CATHERINE TRIO CREMALDI
WITH
DIANE SHERLOCK

ILLUSTRATIONS BY MARILYN CATHCART

Published by Doubleday, a division of Bantam Doubleday Dell Publishing Group, Inc.,
666 Fifth Avenue, New York, New York 10103.

Doubleday and the portrayal of an anchor with a dolphin are trademarks of Doubleday,
a division of Bantam Doubleday Dell Publishing Group, Inc.

DESIGNED BY RHEA BRAUNSTEIN

Library of Congress Cataloging-in-Publication Data

Cremaldi, Catherine Trio.
The Cremaldi cookbook / Catherine Trio Cremaldi with Diane Sherlock; illustrations by Marilyn
Cathcart. — 1st ed.
p.   cm.
Includes index.
1. Cookery, Italian.   I. Sherlock, Diane.   II. Title.
TX723.C696 1988
641.5—dc19   87-21921
CIP

ISBN 0-385-24025-2 Hardbound
0-385-24026-0 Paperbound

With love to . . .

    . . . Gram and Honey, for teaching an eight-year-old girl the joys of cooking

    . . . Mother and Father, for giving me the training and experience of a lifetime

    . . . my husband, Cosmo, my right arm for twenty-seven years, for supporting me always, right or wrong

    . . . and my daughter, Genevieve, "the love of my life," whose enthusiasm has always kept me going

CONTENTS

ACKNOWLEDGMENTS

I HAVE SO MANY SPECIAL PEOPLE TO THANK—FRIENDS, RELATIVES, customers, all of whom have supported me as well as Cremaldi's over the years and many of whom have made unique contributions to this book.

For their continued enthusiasm and constant smiles of encouragement, I'd like to thank: Elisa and Theo Baar, Henry Whittlesey, Phyllis Rubottom, Dr. Graham Blaine, Jimmy De Francisco, Marion (Mickey) Sullivan and former mayor Walter Sullivan, Police Chief Tony Paolillo, Suzanne Jensen, Terri and Dom Scalese, Trish Salvatore, Elsa Dorfman, Tom Tosi, Barbara Haber, Jane and John Boyajian, Maureen and Jim Baker, Jay Gammel, Michael Fitzhugh, Janet Munroe, Tony and Olga Russo, Liz Gallinaro, Chris Halford, Jay Britt, Leona and Jerry Tigar, Leon De Magistris, Mary Colaiuta Lo Curto, and Marcia Sherlock.

I'm especially grateful to the following people, not only for allowing me to use their valued recipes, but also for sharing so much of their family history: Cathy, Toni, and Louie Trio, Jenny Trio Grace, Kiki Boschi Jasiul, Armando Boschi, Frank Bellotti, Laura Ridge, Rosaria, Angelo and Mary Tuccelli, Anna Amentola, Cosmo DiRusso, Lena Pissinis Waldron, Tom Engling, Janice Corea Stack, Joe and Gilda Vulltaggio, Christina and Ted Dierker, Rico De Cenzo, Florence Umberger, Rose Cremaldi Viola, Eleanore Lowery, Janet Reider, and "Babe" Lowery Power.

To the many people at Doubleday who have worked on this book, I'd like to offer my appreciation, with particular thanks to: Les Pockell, Karen Van Westering, and Peter Kruzan.

I also have to offer very special thanks to Marilyn Cathcart, whose lovely drawings adorn these pages. She pulled out all the stops to do the impossible!

Finally, my fondest thanks go to Doe Coover, for keeping after me all these years to write this cookbook—without her it would not have happened; to Lindy Hess Appleton, for her wonderful support, from patronizing Trio's and Cremaldi's to the helpful hints and suggestions throughout this undertaking; and to Diane Sherlock, whose talent for language transformed my family stories, my recipes, and my ideas about cooking into enjoyable prose. Diane's good humor allowed her to put up with me for a year; even family problems and employee crises didn't seem to faze her. Thanks, too, to Paul for waiting those last few days! ◆

THE CREMALDI COOKBOOK

INTRODUCTION

N

O MATTER HOW YOU CUT IT, SUNDAY WAS MACARONI day at our house back in Pennsylvania. As my mother still likes to preach, "No way in God's creation could it have been Sunday without having some kind of macaroni." The morning began when she dusted her old pine table with flour just as she had always seen her mother do. In the center of the table she made a mound of flour and in the middle of the mound she dug a well. There she beat the eggs with her fork and began gathering in the flour, kneading until the texture felt just right. Then with her broomstick handle (yes, her broomstick handle), my mother began to roll.

My mother could transform the most ordinary broomstick handle into a wand of magic. First she would scrub it down hard until the wood shone with a dull, smooth glow. And then, long before there were pasta makers or Cuisinarts, when the only work surface we had was our kitchen table and the only water we could get from the tap was cold, my mother would use that old broomstick to roll out her macaroni dough.

It was always macaroni back then, never pasta or the traditional potato gnocchi or a ravioli stuffed with meat. There were no flavors then either, only egg. Still, when my mother asked us, "What kind of macaroni would you like today?" the possibilities seemed endless. There was lasagna—long, wide yellow noodles that we loved to watch swimming in the pot; the incredibly thin, delicate angel hair; and big squares of dough called spizzigotti that were our favorites.

I learned to cook by watching, just as my mother and grandmother had learned before me. Those two women translated the tastes and traditions their family had brought with them from the mountainous Italian province of Abruzzi to the realities of their new life as the wives of Pennsylvania coal miners. When they were unable to afford shortening, they made their own lard from the fat of a pig the men had slaughtered. Unable to find tender beef, they simmered soups and stocks from their own chickens, with vegetables from their own garden. Often they worked together in my grandmother's kitchen, in the big brick house my grandfather had built on the hill.

It wasn't easy, but we never went hungry. Self-sufficiency was the goal; nothing was ever wasted. Trips to the company store, the only store around, were reserved for items like flour or sugar that the miners couldn't grow themselves. Everything else was made from scratch: I never saw a can in my grandmother's kitchen except those she had canned herself. As for their recipes, they were easy enough to remember without writing down. The ingredients were always fresh. The flavors were clear, full, never spicy—like my grandmother's red sauce, colored by tomatoes so ripe they would split open themselves. It was my father and his family, from Sicily, who added the taste of garlic.

They didn't need to add much else. With just some cabbage, potatoes, beans, and a ham bone thrown in for flavor, for example, my father would boil the most wonderful thick stew. To this day, he will have the butchers in Boston's Italian North End save him prosciutto bones to cook for his "depression day" meal. How to do so much with so little is my father's motto in the kitchen. He's still happy to cover his macaroni with just some crushed garlic and a drizzle of olive oil, what the Italians call *aglio olio*. In our family, we always called this dish "poor man's macaroni"—for someone who can't even afford a real sauce. Maybe that's why we've always pronounced its Italian name "I owe you."

From both sides of the family I learned how to make an elegant meal simply, a simple meal elegant. The secret is knowing a basic recipe and then being willing to experiment. Really, it's just common sense. An extra pinch of this, a handful of that, a mouthful of wine—trying new tastes with what my husband Cosmo calls "Italian measurements." You have to use your own judgment. That's how my cousin Kiki's father created the most delicious chicken dish I know, one day after he walked out of his second wife's house carrying just his spices. It's also how I came to invent the different-flavored pastas and sauces that my parents sell. But before I get into all that, let me tell you about their store.

Actually, the store was the biggest experiment of all. It started one Sunday afternoon over a macaroni dinner several years after we had moved to Massachusetts. My brother Louie suggested, "Why don't we open a ravioli shop?" and just like that my mother said, "All right, we'll try it." She had to borrow the forty dollars she needed to open the store in a shack that was once a shoe cobbler's in East Cambridge. For eight quarters a day she rented refrigeration. Each morning my mother used her broomstick handle to roll out five dozen ravioli on the store's only table. And then my mother waited. And waited.

It took a while, but gradually Genevieve Trio's macaroni store caught on.

Word of mouth, you might say. Some people walked in out of curiosity. Others wanted to enjoy the sweet aroma that filled the shop, of the red sauce bubbling away on my mother's tiny used stove. While my mother cooked, my father sold—he had quit his factory job to help her run the store. And before too long the customers started to tell their friends about Trio's, and all of them started coming back for more.

They came back for one thing and one thing alone, and that was the unique product. The sight and taste of my mother's plumply filled ravioli (bigger than people were accustomed to) had completely won them over. "I feel that I'm making a good homemade macaroni, and that's sufficient," my mother used to say. She was right—it was; it still is.

Today, nearly twenty-five years later, Trio's Ravioli Shoppe has become an institution. In the store, now located in the heart of Boston's famed North End, the rented refrigeration has been replaced by an owner-operated freezer and the broomstick handle with a regular roller. But my mother is still making her macaroni (or pasta, as even she now calls it) just as her mother taught her. My parents work hard—seven days a week, twelve months a year, even some holidays. And the customers line up: local politicians, media celebrities, pilots en route from Boston to San Francisco, neighborhood people, the cast of a Broadway-bound musical, and the members of the Boston Symphony. In fact, their products became so popular that my mother decided to give people throughout New England the opportunity to enjoy it. Trio's packaged pasta and sauces were soon sold in more than seventy area supermarkets, and the national market wasn't far behind.

At Trio's, I continued to learn by watching my mother cook, just as I had as a child. But at the store I also took on creative responsibilities, tasting, testing, participating. Cosmo worked too, with customers at the counter, and so did our daughter, Genevieve, who learned to roll the dough just the way her great-grandmother had. For years that dough was always egg-noodle, and the only sauce we sold was my parents' traditional (now famous) red. And it might have stayed that way indefinitely if it hadn't been for the pesto.

Actually, it wasn't the sauce itself, which we had learned to make at the suggestion of some of our Genovese customers, that changed our tastes forever. It was the sweet bite, the mysterious afterglow, and mostly the seductive aroma of the fresh basil we used to make it. As we worked that summer, picking off the dark green leaves until our fingers became black, going through case after case filled with the plant, I became addicted. Pesto wasn't enough for me. I started adding basil to soups, salads, roasts, everything. What I really wanted to find was a food that could capture that irresistible herb perfectly. I didn't have to look farther than the macaroni I was making. And so, one day, I chopped and combined the deep green leaves with some yellow egg dough. A new era had begun.

Basil pasta was soon followed by carrot, asparagus, and artichoke. My mother got into the act too, creating beet pasta, followed by whole wheat, tomato, even lobster. Each morning we posted the macaroni of the day in the store window. The customers loved it. Where else could they find every flavor of pasta imaginable and, what's more, the sauces to match? "We just came up with this Lemon Scallop Sauce to go on top of the lemon pasta," or "This Alfredo is wonderful on chocolate fettuccini," or "Try the Ginger-Vermouth on the carrot and let me know what you think," was how we would introduce our latest innovations. During those first few months of our little revolution, we gave away more than one free container of sauce.

Before too long, though, my father started selling almost as much of my basil as his egg-noodle pasta, and although nothing could ever replace his red sauce, spinach-nut, parsley, gorgonzola, and others were becoming increasingly popular. Cosmo and I were ready to go off on our own. With the right Cambridge location found and a daily macaroni order from Trio's guaranteed, Cremaldi's, a neighborhood store, was born. The family tradition had returned, with a difference.

From the day it opened, Cremaldi's has been more successful than we would ever have dreamed. Maybe that's because the store has always appealed to people who are as diverse as the products that we sell. An elderly Italian lady who lives up the street, a well-known civil liberties lawyer, a management consultant who's hooked on our Spinach-Ricotta Gnocchi, and Cambridge's Mayor Sullivan are among the longtime Cremaldi's regulars. And then there are the many little children, last but certainly never least in our eyes, who come for lunch and stories from my husband, Cosmo.

Many others have also shopped in our store these past few years, including one woman whom I, like many cooks, consider special. She came in during our first summer on a day when I was feeling very overworked—there were customers to wait on and orders to get out, and the bread dough on my table was just not behaving. There I was, covered with flour, my hands sticking to everything, when suddenly I looked up to find Julia Child at our counter along with her husband, Paul. I was so excited that it took me a minute before I could compose myself enough to put down the dough, extend a very floury hand, and stammer out my welcome and appreciation.

But no matter who is in our store, whether it is a professor planning an intimate dinner or a student attempting to reassure his mother back in Iowa that he's eating well, all of our customers know they will always find wonderful food, beautifully prepared and presented, at Cremaldi's. They've also come to look for, even to expect, what's unexpected—the new, the deliciously different, the unique in our cooking. Through our foods, people can share the same sense of discovery and joy that I first experienced in my mother's kitchen back in Pennsylvania. ◆

Italian horn

TRIO'S AND CREMALDI'S ARE NOT ONLY INFORMED FOOD marketplaces; they are also marketplaces for food information. Over the years we must have shared enough cooking methods, helpful hints, and ingredients with our customers to fill an encyclopedia. How long to cook homemade macaroni, where to store fresh herbs, what our scrod is stuffed with, which supermarkets sell Trio's packaged pasta, and what to serve at a cocktail party are all questions we answer on an average day. Of course we've learned from our customers too, not just about the new goat cheese from upstate New York or how our Cornish hens in lemon garlic sauce tasted last night, but also about a dish they came across in their travels or a dessert they'd like us to duplicate.

Surprisingly, though, amid all this free exchange, this constant daily communication, one element has been missing: time. Most of us can think of many places we'd rather spend that all too precious commodity these days than alone in our kitchen. Gone are the days when our only obligation, like my mother's, was to the evening meal. This is an unfortunate development, in my opinion. There is nothing so welcoming for a family to come home to at the end of the day as the smell of something cooking on the stove. Instinctively, we all warm to the goodness of home cooking. Starting from scratch, using only the freshest ingredients available, letting the full flavors come through— this is how we want to feed our families and what we want to eat ourselves. And so we are faced with a dilemma, forced to sacrifice the quality of our cooking to the quantity of time we have available. Or so we think.

In fact, the situation and the opportunity are not mutually exclusive. You can make great fresh homemade foods elegantly, yet simply. Why invest in a pasta maker or even a drying rack when you can make a better product, with hardly any kneading, right on your own kitchen table? Why spend hours laboring over a tomato sauce when you can perfect one in a matter of minutes? Or why search for exotic herbs and spices when you can season a succulent roast chicken with just some parsley, coarse black pepper, and dried rosemary you probably already have in the house? This book will show you how easy and enjoyable truly great cooking can be.

Of course, not everyone will be immediately convinced. Cooking today has become too much of an exacting science and not enough of a creative art. Precise measurements have replaced my mother's handfuls and pinches. Among all the tools, timing, and technique, we've lost the excitement of experimenting, innovating, discovering. We've forgotten that all it really takes to succeed in the kitchen is intuition, judgment, and common sense. If you prefer a particular dish a little hotter or a little less salty, don't let a list of ingredients or instructions prevent you from making the necessary changes. Or if you'd like to try combining some appealing flavors in a new way, why shouldn't you? That's how I invented many of my recipes, ranging from sweet chocolate lasagna to the sauce I call Ginger-Vermouth.

It doesn't take special equipment to be a cook either. We consumers seem to have been convinced that the more clutter we have in our kitchens, the better our food will turn out. My grandmother did all her peeling, cutting, and slicing with one knife that my grandfather sharpened for her on their cement wall. With the snap of her wrist, she transformed a metal fork into a wire whisk. Maybe it's because of her that I still open cans with a knife and always compensate for my chronic shortage of lids for my pots and pans by improvising with whatever plate, board, or skillet is nearest at hand.

There are, however, a few basic ingredients and tools I like to have in my kitchen. The following is a list of what they are and how I use them. I don't think you'll find this list either intimidating or inhibiting. Rather, as you read the book you'll be impressed, as my family always is, by how much can be done with so little.

INGREDIENTS

OIL

Many Italian cookbooks instruct readers to settle for nothing less than extra virgin olive oil. You can buy the best if you'd like, but for frying I almost always find that an oil with a ten percent olive content, or even a plain vegetable oil like Wesson or Crisco, is sufficient. On those rare occasions when the food needs the fragrant, fruity warmth of an olive oil, I specify that in the individual recipe. Otherwise, use whatever vegetable oil appeals to you.

FLOUR

While some cooks feel that the type of flour they use can dramatically alter the texture and taste of a dish, I've always found that an all-purpose unbleached flour works best for macaroni, breads, pizza, pies, and, in fact, all my cooking. To read more about flours, see the introduction to the next chapter, Homemade Macaroni.

TOMATOES

My grandmother never cooked with a tomato, fresh or canned, that she hadn't grown herself. Nowadays few of us can rely on tomatoes from our own gardens; fortunately, there are some good substitutes. In season, I like to buy very ripe plum tomatoes, or sometimes another variety if the particular shipment looks red and juicy. The rest of the year, canned imported Italian tomatoes are my preference because they are riper and sweeter and have a thicker juice than other canned tomatoes currently on the market.

CHEESES

Hard Cheeses:

When one of my grandmother's recipes called for cheese, she always mixed in a Romano. Today I like to sprinkle this sharp and salty cheese from southern Italy on top of many of my foods and rely on it as a basis for some sauces like pesto and Alfredo. Many stores are now selling Pecorino Romano, a cheese made from sheep's milk that is top of the line. Locatelli is another high-quality genuine Romano cheese and is less salty.

For me, the most versatile of cheeses is Parmigiano Reggiano. I love this sweet and mild cow's milk cheese from the region around Parma. When one of my recipes calls for Parmesan, I hope you will use Reggiano.

It's a good idea to buy chunks of the hard cheeses and grate them with an old-fashioned four-sided grater or in a food processor. That's the way to get the full flavor. Whatever you do, make sure your grated cheese is shredded coarsely rather than ground to a fine powder that will simply disappear into your food.

Melting Cheeses:

As for mozzarella, there's more to the stringy cheese than what kids pull off the top of pizza. I use the processed American variety, either whole-milk or part skim, for lasagnas and other baking because although it's more rubbery, it's also more flavorful. Eaten uncooked, it makes for a good snack food, and it's wonderful fried in a teaspoonful of oil as I often do at home: When the mozzarella starts to melt in the skillet, place a slice of bread on top. Swirl the bread around the pan, then pick it up. In practically no time, you have a nourishing open-faced melted cheese sandwich.

Mozzarella di bufala, or buffalo-milk mozzarella, is an authentic mozzarella made from the milk of Mediterranean water buffalo raised on ranches to the south and west of Naples. White in color, usually sold in ovals the shape of large eggs, and packed in brine to prevent spoilage, buffalo-milk mozzarella is highly perishable. It has only a very slight flavor. You can use it on pizza or serve it in a popular salad. (See the chapter Vegetables Hot and Cold.)

Fresh cow's milk mozzarella is made from cow's milk in the United States and served the same way as buffalo mozzarella.

Instead of mozzarella, which wasn't available to us, my family always used scamorza, a good substitute. Maybe that's because my grandmother was from the province of Abruzzi, where this pungently flavored cheese is most popular. Scamorza is hard to find in supermarkets here but usually can be purchased in Italian gourmet shops.

Provolone comes in two varieties: one is soft, sliceable, and semi-sharp; the other is drier, chunked rather than sliced, and very sharp. The dry, sliceable provolone is good for melting. The sharp version is addictive and absolutely delicious eaten plain or in a sandwich or grated over macaroni.

The sharp and creamy Italian fontina, or fontina d'Aosta, also melts beautifully on top of pizza or veal. Look for this semi-hard cheese to have a thin, natural light brown outer rind. Avoid the French, Danish, and Swedish versions of the cheese, which can all be recognized by their red rinds and are much less flavorful than the Italian original.

Soft Cheeses:

Increasingly popular goat cheeses are strong, and smell and taste slightly moldy. There are Italian, French, and domestic types, some of which are dry and some of which are creamy. Goat cheeses vary in appearance too; some are coated with herbs while others are loaded with pepper or covered with ash. I like the domestic goat cheeses because they tend to have a milder flavor and creamier consistency that is good for cooking and spreading.

Whole or skim milk ricotta may look a lot like cottage cheese, but it's much milder and more spreadable. The most common way to use ricotta is in macaroni dishes like stuffed shells, or in some desserts. Growing up, I often had homemade ricotta spread on Italian bread, a treat that has become my daughter's favorite snack. I'd bet most kids would love it.

Mascarpone is a double-cream, very mild Italian cream cheese that is also great to spread on various breads or rolls. Most frequently an ingredient in uncooked desserts, mascarpone is also an irresistible accompaniment to jams. Look for it in specialty shops.

PEPPER

I like my black pepper whole or coarsely ground or crushed with a meat mallet. Pretty pink peppercorns, once the subject of some controversy for the reaction they cause some people, also play an important role in some macaroni and main dishes, as does the hotter crushed red pepper. Use them all for flavor as well as for color.

SALT

Although salt rarely receives the credit it deserves, sometimes it's the secret ingredient in a recipe. Any good cook should know that adding just a little bit of salt improves the taste of many dishes.

HERBS

In summer, when fresh herbs are plentiful, you can freeze them with wonderful results. Place the herb—sliced, chopped, or left whole—in a freezer bag. Seal the bag tightly and you can leave it in the freezer indefinitely. Whenever you need the herb, reach into the bag and break off only what you will use immediately. This way you can enjoy the luxuries of summer year-round.

I always try to keep fresh basil and parsley around, because I find myself using one or the other in just about every dish I make. For fresh parsley, always get the flat (Italian) variety, as it has more flavor than the curly kind. Dried parsley is made from the curly type.

As for other dried herbs and spices, here's a list of those that you can always find in my kitchen:

basil	garlic powder	paprika
bay leaves	whole and ground nutmeg	dried parsley
cinnamon	minced onion	crushed red pepper
cloves	oregano	rosemary

And here are some less common herbs and spices that I find are also nice to have in the house:

allspice	mace
anise seed	marjoram
whole or ground cardamom	mint
cayenne pepper	dry mustard
celery seed or celery salt	pink peppercorns
chervil	poultry seasoning
chili powder	whole sage
whole or ground cumin	Szechwan peppercorn powder
curry powder	sesame seed
dill seed and dill weed	tarragon
fennel seed	turmeric
ginger (both fresh gingerroot and powdered ginger)	white pepper

GARLIC

Garlic also keeps nicely, either frozen or in the refrigerator. To read more about garlic, and my early and continuing romance with it, see the chapter on garlic.

COMMERCIAL OR DRIED PASTA

There are times when it's better to use a commercial rather than a home-made pasta. When convenience or time itself is a factor, or when a recipe calls for a tubular-shaped macaroni like elbows or penne, head for a store rather than your Cuisinart.

Shop for your dried pasta as carefully as you shop for fruits and vegetables. Look for an egg pasta whose color is almost yellow. Pasta made without eggs is whiter. Don't buy a pasta that looks too white or cracked on the surface—it means the dough was old or reprocessed or both. There are also some delicious dried whole-wheat and spinach pastas now being imported from Italy.

Cooking times for dried pasta vary. There is, however, at least one reliable way to tell whether or not it's done. After the water has returned to a boil and the pasta has begun to swim freely in the pot, let it cook for a few minutes. Then cut a strand or piece in half. If there's still a white dot in the middle, the pasta needs to cook a little longer.

BAKING INGREDIENTS

In addition to oil and flour, here is a list of ingredients that should always be on hand if you like to bake:

butter (freeze)	vanilla extract
eggs	dry yeast
white and brown sugar	unsweetened chocolate squares (freeze)
confectioners' sugar	chocolate chips (freeze)
baking powder	raisins (freeze)
baking soda	walnuts (freeze)
cream of tartar	coconut (freeze)

WINES

I like to use the same wines for drinking and cooking. This preference may be a hangover (no pun intended) from the days when the only wines we knew were those my grandfather made in his basement. I can still remember the bunches of light and dark grapes waiting in crates and the people who came to his dining room to sip and to buy. In fact, I even have a watch that one customer gave to my grandmother in lieu of payment for all the wine he drank.

On a more practical and less nostalgic note, however, I have never found that much difference between a more and a less expensive bottle of wine. Besides, isn't what goes into your food as important as what you drink from your glass?

EQUIPMENT

SKILLETS

Also known as frying or sautéing pans, a skillet is an indispensable item in my kitchen. I prefer cooking with a cast-iron skillet because although it takes longer to heat, it retains that heat evenly. Besides, the metal won't ever warp. The 8- and 10-inch are, I find, the most useful skillet sizes. Buy your skillets at a restaurant supplier, if you can, where the quality and the prices are best.

POT

A large, 10-quart pot is what you'll need for making soups and for boiling macaroni in a sufficient amount of water. I prefer pots made of stainless steel because they're lightweight yet durable.

DUTCH OVEN

This often underrated deep-dish casserole is extremely versatile. Use it for simmering sauces, stews, or any other dish that requires slow, even heating.

ROASTING PAN

It doesn't matter whether it's made of clay, pyrex, or whatever, but you'll certainly need a medium-sized deep roaster if you don't already have one. For small roasts, you can probably substitute a lasagna pan.

COOKIE SHEET

You just can't make a bread, pizza, or calzone without a cookie sheet. Buy one that is thick, not flimsy, because the thin ones tend to burn the food.

MIXING BOWLS

Working with a large mixing bowl that is wide as well as deep becomes especially important when you are incorporating ingredients by hand. For making bread dough or for mixing large amounts of ingredients, a bowl 18 inches in diameter is virtually essential; medium-sized bowls are good for mixing smaller amounts.

KNIVES

Three knives will cover all the cutting you'll ever need to do in your kitchen: an 8- or 10-inch chef's knife for chopping, a 3- or 4-inch paring knife for peeling vegetables, and an 8-inch serrated knife for slicing breads or trimming artichokes. Knives made of stainless steel are best.

RUBBER SPATULA

This tool is a great convenience for scraping batters and sauces out of bowls and pots.

WHISK

When I discovered a whisk after years of watching my grandmother and mother beat with a fork, I was ecstatic. In fact, I became so infatuated with whisks, which are faster for mixing than any wooden fork or spoon could ever be, that I began to collect them—big ones, little ones, even miniature ones. Used primarily to incorporate ingredients for sauces that might otherwise lump up, a whisk can almost take the place of an electric mixer. Everyone should own at least a medium one; this size is the most manageable and gives you the greatest control.

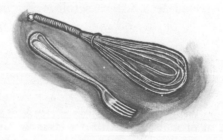

FOOD PROCESSOR

My first encounter with a food processor was in a department store. When I saw everything the machine could do, I was amazed. "Why didn't I invent something like this?" I asked myself. I bought one on the spot and enrolled immediately in a food processor cooking course. For the next year my family ate grated carrots and cole slaw, or what Cosmo refers to as my food processor cuisine.

And what can I say today about a tool that enables me to prepare just about any kind of dish from macaroni through desserts? This is the most useful piece of equipment in my kitchen. Of all the types currently available, I prefer a Cuisinart.

ROLLING PIN

Glass, marble, and long wooden rolling pins without handles are all attractive but, in my opinion, somewhat impractical. A heavy wooden pin with ball-bearing handles can outperform any of the others, by giving you added control and agility.

Although basic, none of these tools or ingredients is an absolute necessity. After all, this book is written for any cook who, when caught without a rolling pin, is willing to turn, as my mother did, to the broomstick. ◆

HOMEMADE MACARONI

"**Y**_____ OU CAN MAKE IT AS GOOD, BUT YOU CAN'T MAKE IT any better." That's how my brother Louie Trio describes the process and the product our family is noted for: homemade macaroni. In this chapter, we'll share for the first time the simple steps behind this well-kept family secret. When you taste the results—thick, chewy, incredibly flavorful—you'll agree that the proof of Louie's statement is in the pasta.

"Pasta," by the way, which means paste or dough in Italian, wasn't a word in my family's vocabulary for years. Instead, we always used the old-fashioned term "macaroni" to describe the entire range of flour-and-egg combinations ranging from the longest, thinnest linguini to the widest spizzigotti or maltagliati to fat ravioli stuffed with cheese. Macaroni was, after all, what the medieval Venetians first named the noodle dish they enjoyed with butter and cheese. And it was as macaroni that Thomas Jefferson introduced the European specialty to America. And a century later, Americans were calling their new "discovery," spaghetti, "a variety of macaroni" as it, along with other noodle dishes, was fast becoming a favorite American food. I don't know why so many people now call it pasta. In our store, I go with the times and use the words "pasta" and "macaroni" interchangeably. But in the book I will use only "macaroni" when referring to that which is homemade, purest, and best.

These days there's usually less fanfare about the name than about the kind of flour used for macaroni dough. Some cooks swear by hard wheat, also known as durum or semolina, while others prefer the more pliable all-purpose flour. I, for one, have never understood what all the fuss is about. The quality of your macaroni is not much affected by the kind of flour you use. For the record, my grandmother, my mother, and I have always preferred an all-purpose flour, partly because that's what each of us grew up with and partly because it seems to produce a macaroni with more body. But what really matters in homemade macaroni making is not which flour you choose, it's how you handle the dough.

Maybe that's why I've never cared for the recently popularized pasta machines: the consistency of dough is different when it's extruded. As my brother would say, pasta produced this way has no bite; there's nothing to sink your teeth into. You put a few slippery strands in your mouth and whoops, they're gone, you missed them. So if you have a pasta machine that you like to use, I'm afraid our basic macaroni recipe won't be much help. Borrow freely from our flavors later in this chapter, but follow your own manufacturer's directions. Just be aware as you're struggling to get your pasta machine clean that you will have missed out on a lot of fun, not to mention the best home-made macaroni you ever tasted.

If you're at the other extreme, however, a traditionalist, satisfied only by the taste and texture of a macaroni made on your table, then use my mother's old-fashioned procedure. Start by placing about two and a half cups of flour in a mound on the table. In the middle of the mound, make a well. Then break four eggs into the well and beat them with a fork. Gather in small amounts of flour as you beat, scraping it from the walls of the well. Then, when the eggs are no longer runny, slowly knead in the rest of the flour, using your palms. Keep kneading in the flour until the dough forms a ball that doesn't crumble or stick to your hands. Add a couple of drops of water if the dough is too

To mix the eggs into the well of flour, rotate the fork around the perimeter of the well, gathering in more flour as you go.

crumbly or a little more flour if the dough is too sticky. Make your macaroni this way and after a few times you'll know by the feel when the texture of the dough is just right.

My mother's "well" is the source of wonderful macaroni. But for most of us today, her method takes too much time and trouble. There is a way, however, to maximize her results while minimizing our efforts. The Basic Homemade Macaroni that follows is the modern version of my mother's traditional family recipe. It, too, makes one to one and a half pounds of good rich homemade egg macaroni and will serve four to six people. The rest of the recipes in this chapter, with all the wacky and wonderful flavors we've invented, are variations on this basic macaroni theme, followed by our sauce recommendations at the end of the chapter. All you'll need to begin are a food processor, a heavy rolling pin (preferably one with ball bearings), a sharp knife, and a little common sense to make our family recipe your own. ◆

BASIC HOMEMADE MACARONI

Makes 1–1½ pounds macaroni; serves 4–6

1. In a food processor fitted with the steel blade, combine the flour and the eggs. Process for 40 seconds. During this time, the dough first will look like coarse meal and then should form a ball. This ball should stick together but should not stick to your hands. Sometimes the dough does not form a ball with the right consistency after 40 seconds of processing. Here are three common problems you may encounter and what to do about them:

2½ cups flour
4 eggs

• The dough may form a layer under or over the steel blade, instead of a ball. In this case, test the dough by squeezing a little in your hand. If the dough sticks together but does not stick to your hand, then turn it out on a lightly floured surface and form it into a nice, neat ball yourself. Resume the recipe with step 3.
• The dough may be too dry. If the dough doesn't stick together and starts to crumble, then add 1 teaspoon of water and process again for 10 more seconds. The dough should now form a ball with the right consistency. If it doesn't, then add more water, a teaspoon at a time, and process again until the dough comes together.
• The dough may be too wet. If the dough is too sticky, then add 1 tablespoon of flour and process again for 10 more seconds. The dough

should now form a ball with the right consistency. If it doesn't, then add up to 3 tablespoons more flour, a tablespoon at a time, and process again until the dough is no longer sticky.

2. When the dough stays together without being too dry or too sticky, turn it out on a lightly floured surface. Knead the dough briefly until it forms a nice, neat ball. (The dough is already half kneaded by the food processor. Kneading much more would make the dough too smooth and shiny, creating a macaroni without a distinctive texture.) If you'd like to make the dough more pliable, let it rest under an inverted bowl for about 10 minutes after kneading.

Knead the dough only briefly until it forms a ball.

3. Using a heavy rolling pin, roll out the dough into a rough circle or oval about 23 inches in diameter and 1/8 inch in thickness (the thickness of a nickel). Put a lot of pressure on the rolling pin to stretch out the dough. Aim to get the right, even thickness for the dough rather than a perfect shape.

4. Fold the circle or oval of dough like a jelly roll. Using a sharp knife, cut the roll crosswise, slicing the macaroni into strands of your desired width. Thinner strips will yield spaghetti or linguini; wider ones will yield fettuccini or lasagna, which can be cut again into the diamond-shaped spizzigotti or maltagliati. Cut your dough as thin as your knife will let you or as wide as you need it. (To shape ravioli and other filled macaronis, please see the introduction to the next chapter.)

5. After the whole roll is sliced, take it apart by gently unraveling each strand of macaroni and piling the separated strands in a small mound. Sprinkle an additional 1/4 cup flour over the macaroni and toss the strands (or "ruffle them up" as we like to say in my family) with your hands.

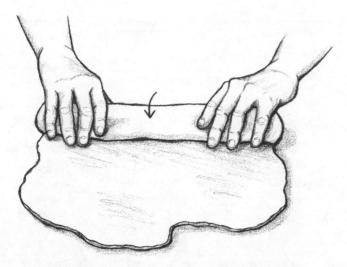

After the dough is rolled out to a circle 23 inches in diameter and ⅛ inch thick, flour the surface lightly and fold the dough over like a jelly roll.

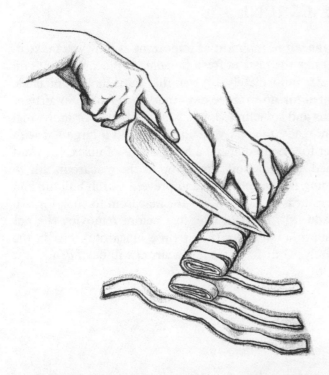

Slice the dough roll according to the type of macaroni you want. You can make skinny spaghetti strands or wide lasagna noodles—and anything in between!

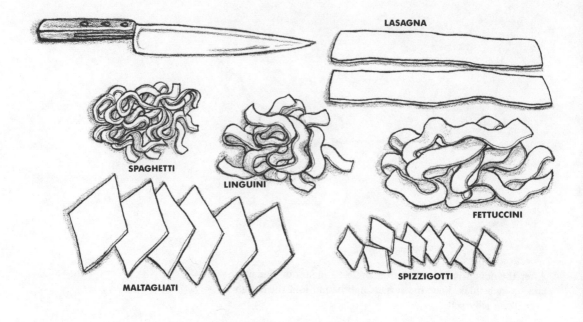

LASAGNA

SPAGHETTI

LINGUINI

FETTUCCINI

MALTAGLIATI

SPIZZIGOTTI

HOW TO COOK MACARONI

How you cook your macaroni is almost as important as how you make it. Of course, there's nothing like the taste of fresh homemade macaroni, but you don't have to boil your water immediately, or even that same day. Homemade macaroni can be refrigerated for up to three days (and even frozen in airtight bags for up to three months and sometimes longer) in half-pound or individual portions. Whenever you're ready to cook your macaroni, fill a large pot with at least five quarts of water for one to one and a half pounds of macaroni. Wait until the water has reached a rolling boil, then drop in the macaroni. Stir to keep the macaroni swimming freely in the pot and prevent starch buildup and sticking. When the water returns to a boil, allow the macaroni to cook for two more minutes. You can add salt, if you'd like, just before removing the pot from the stove. Then drain in a collander (never rinse macaroni), mix in the sauce, and serve immediately. Your homemade macaroni will be *al dente,* just the way my family likes it.

BASIL MACARONI

Makes 1–1½ pounds macaroni; serves 4–6

This innocent-looking speckled macaroni inspired me to invent all the other flavors. It happened one day when I chopped deep green leaves into some yellow egg dough at my parents' store and discovered a way to capture the sweet bite and mysterious afterglow of basil inside a wholesome food. Could carrot, red pepper, or even chocolate have been far behind? Surprisingly, I've since found out through experimentation that dried basil is even more flavorful for macaroni making than the fresh herb.

In a food processor fitted with the steel blade, combine the flour, eggs, and dried basil. Then follow the rest of the instructions for Basic Homemade Macaroni.

2½ cups flour
4 eggs
2 heaping tablespoons dried basil or 4 tablespoons fresh basil, finely chopped

WHOLE WHEAT MACARONI

Makes 1–1½ pounds macaroni; serves 4–6

Everyday at Cremaldi's we sell a different prepared diet dinner, designed not only for those who are counting calories, but also for those who want an especially nutritious one-dish meal. Many of our customers complement these dinners by serving them on a bed of pasta. Whole wheat macaroni is perfect for such an important supporting role.

In a food processor fitted with the steel blade, combine the whole wheat flour and the eggs. Then follow the rest of the instructions for Basic Homemade Macaroni.

2½ cups whole wheat flour
4 eggs

SPINACH MACARONI

Makes 1–1½ pounds macaroni; serves 4–6

What better way to feed your child a nourishing bowl of spinach without his knowing it? Not to mention that adults, too, find this a particularly appealing way to get their nutrients.

1. In a food processor fitted with the steel blade, combine the spinach and eggs. Process until puréed.

2. Add the flour, and process again, following the rest of the instructions for Basic Homemade Macaroni.

4 cups fresh spinach, cleaned and loosely packed in measuring cup

4 eggs

2½ cups flour

TOMATO MACARONI

Makes 1–1½ pounds macaroni; serves 4–6

When a red sauce isn't enough . . .

In a food processor fitted with the steel blade, combine the flour, eggs, and tomato paste. Then follow the rest of the instructions for Basic Homemade Macaroni.

2½ cups flour

4 eggs

2 tablespoons tomato paste

CARROT MACARONI

Makes 1–1½ pounds macaroni; serves 4–6

Did you know that carrots make you see in the dark and your hair turn curly? You may not believe carrots can do these things, but you will believe carrot macaroni!

In a food processor fitted with the steel blade, combine the flour, eggs, and cooked carrots. Then follow the rest of the instructions for Basic Homemade Macaroni.

2½ cups flour

4 eggs

1½ cups cooked carrots, cut in 2-inch pieces

ASPARAGUS MACARONI

Makes 1–1½ pounds macaroni; serves 4–6

You can still taste the delicate tips and tender stems in this glorious golden green macaroni. Top it with a cream sauce and you may never go back to asparagus with hollandaise again. Remember to drain the spears well after cooking, as asparagus tends to hold water even more than most vegetables do.

In a food processor fitted with the steel blade, combine the flour, eggs, and cooked asparagus spears. Then follow the rest of the instructions for Basic Homemade Macaroni.

2½ cups flour

4 eggs

1½ cups cooked or canned asparagus spears, cut in 2-inch pieces

ARTICHOKE MACARONI

Makes 1–1½ pounds macaroni; serves 4–6

Like some people, artichokes have tough exteriors but tender hearts. In macaroni, these soft and creamy centers are especially irresistible.

1. Place the artichoke hearts and the eggs in a food processor fitted with the steel blade. Process until pureed.

2. Add the flour to the artichoke hearts and the eggs and process again, following the rest of the instructions for Basic Homemade Macaroni.

8½-ounce can artichoke hearts, drained

2 eggs

4 cups flour

BEET MACARONI

Makes 1–1½ pounds macaroni; serves 4–6

Sometimes it's our customers who inspire us to invent new flavors. That is how my mother came to create beet macaroni. Trio's customers urged her to experiment with it, mainly because of its spectacular raspberry color, and she was happy to comply. The flavor became a regular in her repertoire, despite the fact that whenever she would make it her hands, like the macaroni, turned a bright beet red.

In a food processor fitted with the steel blade, combine the flour, eggs, and cooked beets. Then follow the rest of the instructions for Basic Homemade Macaroni.

2½ cups flour

4 eggs

1½ cups cooked beets (canned or fresh), drained

ZUCCHINI MACARONI

Makes 1–1½ pounds macaroni; serves 4–6

Aren't Italians (and Italian-Americans) the only ones who really know how to cook with this great vegetable? We fry it, bake it, stuff it, purée it into soup, and fold it into batter for bread. In macaroni, zucchini works its magic for us again, producing a magnificent color and a fine, full flavor.

In a food processor fitted with a steel blade, combine the flour, eggs, and cooked zucchini. Then follow the rest of the instructions for Basic Homemade Macaroni.

2½ cups flour

4 eggs

1½ cups cooked zucchini (boiled until tender, about 15 minutes), cut in 2-inch pieces

BLACK PEPPER MACARONI

Makes 1–1½ pounds macaroni; serves 4–6

I love the flavorful crunchiness of coarse black pepper. Often I put peppercorns in a dishtowel, make a knot in it, and then hammer to crush the peppercorns myself. This macaroni is a wonderful way to capture that crunch inside a wholesome food.

In a food processor fitted with the steel blade, combine the flour, eggs, and coarse black pepper. Then follow the rest of the instructions for Basic Homemade Macaroni.

2½ cups flour

4 eggs

2 tablespoons coarsely ground black pepper

PINK PEPPERCORN MACARONI

Makes 1–1½ pounds macaroni; serves 4–6

The appearance and origin of this rose-colored berry from off the coast of Madagascar may be a bit exotic, but the taste of the pink peppercorn has almost universal appeal. Serve this macaroni with a mild white sauce or just some butter and grated Parmesan cheese to really appreciate the beautiful sweet, slightly peppery flavor. And if, like me, you find you can't get enough of its delicate crunch, serve this macaroni with Shrimp with Pink Peppercorn Sauce (p. 189).

1. Place the peppercorns in a plastic bag and crush them with a mallet. (They're soft and will crush easily.)

2. In a food processor fitted with the steel blade, combine the peppercorns, flour, and eggs. Then follow the rest of the instructions for Basic Homemade Macaroni.

⅓ cup pink peppercorns (measure after you crush them)

2½ cups flour

4 eggs

RED PEPPER MACARONI

Makes 1–1½ pounds macaroni; serves 4–6

Don't miss out on this speckled red macaroni because you think it's too hot to handle. The one heaping teaspoon of crushed red pepper the recipe calls for produces a dough that is medium hot, so just use less if you prefer a milder taste. Use your own judgment. And remember, after the macaroni is cooked, a lot of the hotness disappears.

In a food processor fitted with the steel blade, combine the flour, eggs, and red pepper. Then follow the rest of the instructions for Basic Homemade Macaroni.

2½ cups flour
4 eggs
1 heaping teaspoon crushed red pepper

FENNEL MACARONI

Makes 1–1½ pounds macaroni; serves 4–6

My daughter, Genevieve, invented this macaroni when she fell in love with the licorice-like taste of fennel. The ground fennel is used for flavor, the seeds for texture.

In a food processor fitted with the steel blade, combine the flour, eggs, ground fennel, and whole fennel. Then follow the rest of the instructions for Basic Homemade Macaroni.

2½ cups flour
4 eggs
1 heaping tablespoon ground fennel
1 heaping teaspoon whole fennel seed

CHIVE MACARONI

Makes 1–1½ pounds macaroni; serves 4–6

I've always been fascinated by the long, slender green stalks growing in pots sold in the supermarket. I've even bought chives this way sometimes and set them on my windowsill to admire them. But, of course, this member of the onion family offers more than mere appearance to recommend it. In fact, once you experience the flavor of chives in macaroni, I think you'll find it quite unforgettable.

In a food processor fitted with the steel blade, combine the flour, eggs, and chives. Then follow the rest of the instructions for Basic Homemade Macaroni.

2½ cups flour
4 eggs
¼ cup minced freeze-dried or fresh chives

SAGE MACARONI

Makes 1–1½ pounds macaroni; serves 4–6

Why does eating a food seasoned with sage always leave me with a warm and cozy feeling? Maybe it's because when I was a child, the stuffing in our Thanksgiving bird was rich with the savory herb. And now as an adult I can conjure up happy memories by making this macaroni.

In a food processor fitted with the steel blade, combine the flour, eggs, and rubbed sage. Then follow the rest of the instructions for Basic Homemade Macaroni.

2½ cups flour
4 eggs
2 heaping tablespoons rubbed sage

PARSLEY MACARONI

Makes 1–1½ pounds macaroni; serves 4–6

Many people underestimate the full flavor of parsley. That's because they buy the curly parsley, which is strictly for decoration and, in my opinion, has no taste at all. Italian parsley which is flat rather than curly, is the only kind you'll ever find in my kitchen. It turns macaroni bright green, the color of fresh grass.

1. In a food processor fitted with the steel blade, combine the parsley and the eggs. Process briefly until puréed.

2. Add the flour and process again, following the rest of the instructions for Basic Homemade Macaroni.

2 cups Italian parsley leaves
    and tender stems
4 eggs
2½ cups flour

NUTMEG MACARONI

Makes 1–1½ pounds macaroni; serves 4–6

With its festive golden color, this macaroni will light up your holiday table. Wrap the nutmeg strands in a warm cream sauce to fully savor their richness.

In a food processor fitted with the steel blade, combine the flour, eggs, and nutmeg. Then follow the rest of the instructions for Basic Homemade Macaroni.

2½ cups flour
4 eggs
⅓ cup nutmeg

GARLIC MACARONI

Makes 1–1½ pounds macaroni; serves 4–6

Why always save the garlic for the sauce?

1. In a food processor fitted with the steel blade, combine the eggs and the garlic. Process about 10 seconds until the garlic is fine.

2. Add the flour and rosemary to the garlic and eggs. Process again, and then follow the rest of the instructions for Basic Homemade Macaroni.

4 eggs
4 large or 8 small garlic
    cloves, peeled
2½ cups flour
1 heaping tablespoon dried
    rosemary leaves

SAFFRON MACARONI

Makes 1–1½ pounds macaroni; serves 4–6

With all the hard work that goes into picking, separating, and drying the stigmas of the crocus flower to make saffron, it seems a shame that the taste is lost in so many dishes. The problem is that this very expensive spice is easily overwhelmed by other ingredients. But provide it with a simple setting, like macaroni dough, and saffron's unique flavor becomes instantly detectable. In fact, the flavor seems to shine through, like the color of this macaroni, a glorious golden.

1. Mix the saffron and hot water in a cup. Stir and let stand for 5 minutes.

2. In a food processor fitted with the steel blade, combine the mixed saffron, flour, and eggs. Then follow the rest of the instructions for Basic Homemade Macaroni.

1 tablespoon saffron
2 tablespoons hot water
2½ cups flour
4 eggs

LEMON MACARONI

Makes 1–1½ pounds macaroni; serves 4–6

You just can't imagine the exciting flavor until you bite into this chewy macaroni with the strong, refreshing taste of lemon peel. Try it and feel your palate come alive.

1. Place the lemon peels in a food processor fitted with the steel blade. Process until very fine.

2. Add the flour and eggs to the lemon peels and process again, following the rest of the instructions for Basic Homemade Macaroni.

Peels of 2 lemons
2½ cups flour
4 eggs

ORANGE MACARONI

Makes 1–1½ pounds macaroni; serves 4–6

This is one time when you almost certainly will have to add more flour to the dough to compensate for the ingredients' added moisture. But the little bit of extra effort is well worth it. Just wait until you taste the sweet zing of the fresh oranges!

1. Place the orange peels in a food processor fitted with the steel blade. Process until very fine.

2. Add the eggs, flour, and orange juice and process until the dough forms a ball or a layer. If the dough seems too dry, add more orange juice, a teaspoon at a time, and reprocess. If the dough seems too sticky, add more flour, a tablespoon at a time, and reprocess. Now follow the rest of the instructions for Basic Homemade Macaroni.

Peels of 2 oranges
4 eggs
2½ cups flour
Juice of 1 orange

SUN-DRIED TOMATO MACARONI

Makes 1–1½ pounds macaroni; serves 4–6

Americans have been raving about sun-dried tomatoes ever since their salty, shriveled little bodies were first packed in oil and imported from Italy. But everything you've heard about them is faint praise compared to what you'll receive if you make this macaroni for family or friends. I guarantee this dish will be the topic of conversation.

1. In a food processor fitted with the steel blade, combine the tomatoes and the eggs. Process until puréed.

2. Add the flour and process again until the dough forms a ball or a layer. If the dough seems too dry, add more olive oil, a teaspoon at a time, and reprocess. If the dough seems too sticky, add more flour, a tablespoon at a time, and reprocess.

3. Follow the rest of the instructions for Basic Homemade Macaroni.

8 sun-dried tomatoes in olive oil
4 eggs
3½ cups flour

PORT MACARONI

Makes 1–1½ pounds macaroni; serves 4–6

I'm a long-time lover of port, not just in my glass, but also sizzling on my filet mignon or mixed with fruit and Crème Fraîche to create a cool and enticing dessert (see p. 243). So wouldn't port's nutty flavor and deep wine color also make a fabulous macaroni? I asked myself. Of course it would.

1. In a food processor fitted with the steel blade, combine the flour and the eggs. Process, adding the tablespoons of port one at a time, until the dough forms a ball or a layer. If the dough seems too dry, add more port, a teaspoon at a time, and reprocess. If the dough seems too sticky, add more flour, a tablespoon at a time, and reprocess.

2. Follow the rest of the instructions for Basic Homemade Macaroni.

2½ *cups flour*
2 *eggs*
12 *tablespoons port wine*

PROVOLONE MACARONI

Makes 1–1½ pounds macaroni; serves 4–6

Why do we always have to sprinkle cheese on top *of our macaroni?*

1. Place the cheese in a food processor fitted with the steel blade. Process until very fine.

2. Add the flour and eggs to the cheese and process again, following the rest of the instructions for Basic Homemade Macaroni.

½ *pound aged, sharp provolone cheese, cubed*
2½ *cups flour*
3 *eggs*

CHOCOLATE MACARONI

Makes 1–1½ pounds macaroni; serves 4–6

This alluring macaroni is not sweet; it can be eaten as a first course or an entree. Top it with melted butter to taste just a hint of chocolate flavoring. Or bathe the chocolate in an elegant cream sauce, like Alfredo, to create a stunning color combination.

In a food processor fitted with the steel blade, combine the flour, eggs, and cocoa. Then follow the rest of the instructions for Basic Homemade Macaroni.

2½ cups flour
4 eggs
⅓ cup unsweetened cocoa

POTATO GNOCCHI

Serves 4–6

Italians have been eating gnocchi, the little floury dumplings that just melt in your mouth, for centuries. Traditional gnocchi are made with potato, and this is the only way I ever ate them as a child. My mother would rush to mash the potatoes through her ricer when they were still very hot and end up with a real mushy dough that went directly into the garbage. I suspected that the potatoes needed to cool before using the ricer and one day taught my mother a thing or two—I took my time with the potatoes and my gnocchi ended up with a much better texture. I do still hurry once the gnocchi are made, however. That's because all gnocchi must be cooked immediately or fast-frozen, on a cookie sheet, barely touching one another. After they are frozen hard, the gnocchi can be packed in baggies to be left for several days, weeks, or even months in the freezer.

1. Place the potatoes in a pot, cover them with water, and bring the water to a boil. Boil the potatoes until they are thoroughly cooked. Remove the potatoes from the water. Peel them when they are still slightly warm.

2. When the peeled potatoes are cool, purée them in a food processor fitted with the steel blade.

3. Add 2 cups of flour to the puréed potatoes. Process for about 15 seconds or until the flour and potatoes form a soft ball of dough.

4. Turn the dough out on a well-floured surface. Coat the dough with the flour so that the outside of the ball is

1 pound potatoes (6 small or 3 large)

2 cups flour, plus additional flour for rolling

no longer sticky. Then pat the ball of dough into an oval shape.

5. Using a sharp knife, slice the dough like a loaf of bread. Each slice should be about 1½ inches wide.

6. Coat the sticky sides of each slice of dough with more flour. Then, with your hands, roll out each slice to form ropes of dough the thickness of your index finger (or thinner if you prefer). Slice the ropes into ½-inch chunks.

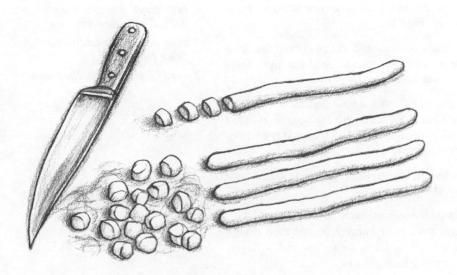

Slice each rope of dough into ½-inch chunks.

7. Immediately coat each chunk with flour. Toss and separate the gnocchi in the flour to prevent them from sticking. Use more flour if necessary. Freeze or cook the gnocchi right away.

8. To cook, bring 6 quarts of cold water to a rolling boil. Shake the excess flour off the gnocchi and drop them into the boiling water. Stir the water vigorously for the first minute. When the water returns to a boil, cook the gnocchi 6–7 minutes or until they float to the surface. (If your gnocchi have been frozen, cook without thawing them first.)

SPINACH-RICOTTA GNOCCHI

My mother-in-law, Rose Viola, introduced me to light, fluffy, ricotta gnocchi. I paired it with one of my favorite vegetables. The resulting combination has become a favorite in our family. We like to serve these gnocchi drenched in a hearty red sauce or mixed with plenty of Parmesan, topped with grated mozzarella, and then baked in a casserole until the cheese melts.

1. Place the spinach in a food processor fitted with the steel blade. Process until fine.

2. Add the 3 cups of flour and the ricotta to the spinach. Process for about 15 seconds or until the ingredients form a soft ball of dough.

3. Turn the dough out onto a well-floured surface and form into a ball. Coat the dough with the flour so that the outside of the ball is no longer sticky. Then pat the ball of dough into an oval shape.

4. Slice the dough like a loaf of bread. Each slice should be about 1½ inches wide.

5. Coat the sticky sides of each slice of dough with more flour. Then, with your hands, roll out each dough slice to form ropes the thickness of your index finger. Slice the ropes into ½ inch chunks.

6. Immediately coat each chunk with flour. Toss and separate the gnocchi in the remaining flour to prevent them from sticking. Use more flour, if necessary. Freeze or cook the gnocchi right away.

7. To cook the gnocchi, bring 6 quarts of water to a rolling boil. Shake the excess flour off the gnocchi and drop them into the boiling water. Stir the water vigorously for the first minute. When the water returns to a boil, cook the gnocchi 6–7 minutes or until they float to the surface. (If your gnocchi have been frozen, cook without thawing them first.)

4 cups fresh spinach, loosely packed in measuring cup

3 cups flour, plus additional flour for rolling

2 cups (1 pound) ricotta cheese

ORANGE-RICOTTA GNOCCHI

Serves 4–6

The orange peel lends the most refreshing flavor to these gnocchi while the ricotta gives the texture an added bounce. A good dish to serve year-round.

1. Place the orange peel in a food processor fitted with the steel blade. Process until very fine.

2. Add 4 cups flour and the ricotta to the orange peel. Process for about 15 seconds or until the ingredients form a ball.

3. Turn the dough out on a well-floured surface. Coat the dough with the flour so that the outside of the ball is no longer sticky. Then pat the ball of dough into an oval shape.

4. Slice the dough like a loaf of bread. Each slice should be about 1½ inches wide.

5. Coat the sticky sides of each slice of dough with more flour. Then, with your hands, roll out each dough slice to form ropes the thickness of your index finger. Slice the ropes into ½ inch chunks.

6. Immediately coat each chunk with flour. Toss and separate the gnocchi in the flour to prevent them from sticking. Use more flour, if necessary. Freeze or cook the gnocchi right away.

7. To cook the gnocchi, bring 6 quarts of cold water to a rolling boil. Shake the excess flour off the gnocchi and drop them into the boiling water. Stir the water vigorously for the first minute. When the water returns to a boil, cook the gnocchi 6–7 minutes or until they float to the surface. (If your gnocchi have been frozen, cook without thawing them first.)

Peel of 1 large orange
4 cups flour, plus additional flour for rolling
2 cups (1 pound) ricotta cheese

SQUASH GNOCCHI

Food ideas flow both ways across the Atlantic. With sun-dried tomatoes, pesto, fontina cheese, and the like, it would be easy to conclude that we Americans are the sole beneficiaries of our continual culinary exchange with Italy, but in fact Italian cooks occasionally borrow from us, too. This is certainly the case with squash and pumpkin, two vegetables the Italians even refer to as "American." Here's a delicious treat that Italians make with our native squash, an ingredient they import rather than growing it themselves.

1. If you're using fresh squash, boil it until well done and drain. When the squash is cold, place it in a food processor fitted with the steel blade. Process until puréed, then add the other ingredients to the processor. If you're using canned squash, place all the ingredients in the food processor at the same time.

2. Process the squash, flour, cinnamon, and nutmeg for about 15 seconds, or until the ingredients form a soft ball of dough.

3. Turn the dough out onto a well-floured surface. Coat the dough with the flour so that the outside of the ball is no longer sticky. Then pat the ball of dough into an oval shape.

4. Slice the dough like a loaf of bread. Each slice should be about 1½ inches wide.

5. Coat the sticky sides of each slice of dough with more flour. Then, with your hands, roll out each dough slice to form ropes the thickness of your index finger. Slice the ropes into ½ inch chunks.

6. Immediately coat each chunk with flour. Toss and separate the gnocchi in the flour to prevent them from sticking. Use more flour if necessary. Freeze or cook the gnocchi right away.

7. To cook the gnocchi, bring 6 quarts of cold water to a rolling boil. Shake the excess flour off the gnocchi and drop them into the boiling water. Stir the water vigorously for the first minute. When it returns to a boil, cook the gnocchi 6–7 minutes or until they float to the surface. (If your gnocchi have been frozen, cook without thawing them first.)

2 cups fresh butternut squash, peeled and cut into chunks, or 15 ounces canned squash

3 cups flour, plus additional flour for rolling

1 teaspoon ground cinnamon

1 teaspoon ground nutmeg

CREMALDI'S RECOMMENDS

While you can pair any flavor macaroni with any sauce that seems fitting to you, we do have a few favorite combinations I'd like to share. Listed below are all the flavors of macaroni described in this chapter; next to each are a few sauces we feel best complement the macaroni. But remember that in my kitchen creativity is next to godliness! So go wild and create your own favorite mix-and-match meals.

MACARONI	SAUCES
Egg Noodle	Any sauce
Garlic	Sun-dried Tomato, Parsley, Calamari, 15-Minute Tomato
Spinach	Calamari, Spinach-Nut, Alfredo, Famous Tomato, Sauce for Straw and Hay
Pink Peppercorn	Alfredo, Prosciutto Cream, Butter and Cream
Nutmeg	Broccoli Cream, Butter and Cream, Alfredo
Basil	Gaeta, Pesto, any tomato sauce, Crème Fraîche
Tomato	Cherry Tomato Cream, Parsley, Sun-dried Tomato, Pesto
Carrot	Bolognese, Ginger-Vermouth, Smoked Scallop, Spinach-Nut
Asparagus	Ginger-Vermouth, Porcini, Prosciutto Cream
Beet	Tuna, Alfredo, Spinach-Nut
Orange	Anchovy Pine-Nut Currant, Smoked Scallop, Crème Fraîche
Whole Wheat	Porcini, Sesame Butter, Tomato-Vegetable, 15-Minute Tomato
Parsley	Anchovy-Pine Nut-Currant, White Clam, Real Fast Meat Sauce, Parsley, Tuna
Zucchini	Bolognese, Porcini, Ginger-Vermouth, any tomato sauce, Calamari
Sage	Gorgonzola, Crème Fraîche, Butter and Cream
Chive	Bolognese, Butter and Cream, Gaeta, Cherry Tomato Cream
Port	Anchovy-Pine Nut-Currant, Tomato-Vegetable, 15-Minute Tomato, Orange, Butter and Cream

Sun-dried Tomato	Gaeta, Tuna, Spinach-Nut, Sun-dried Tomato
Provolone	Crème Fraîche, Smoked Scallop, any tomato sauce
Saffron	Cherry Tomato Cream, Gorgonzola, Cream and Butter
Lemon	Calamari, Lo-Cal Tomato, Lemon Scallop, Pesto
Black Pepper	Famous Tomato, Crème Fraîche, White Clam
Red Pepper	Tuna, Cherry Tomato Cream, Ginger-Vermouth, Gaeta
Chocolate	Alfredo, Orange, Butter and Cream
Fennel	Porcini, Tuna, Gaeta, any tomato sauce
Artichoke	Cherry Tomato Cream, Crème Fraîche, any red sauce, Butter and Cream

GNOCCHI

Potato Gnocchi	Any tomato sauce
Spinach-Ricotta Gnocchi	Any tomato sauce, Spinach-Nut, Gorgonzola
Orange-Ricotta Gnocchi	Crème Fraîche, Orange, Anchovy-Pine Nut-Currant
Squash Gnocchi	Famous Tomato, Alfredo

Cheese-
Filled
Tortellini

Salmon-
Filled
Agnolotti

Pesto-
Filled
Raviolini

I N THE PAST, IF YOU KNEW WHAT REGION OF ITALY A PERSON came from you could pretty well guess what type of filled macaroni he served at his table. People from the area around Bologna known as Emilia-Romagna, for instance, took pride in their tortelloni, tortellini, and cappelletti, while as the child of an Abruzzi family, the only filled macaroni I ever ate was ravioli stuffed with meat. Big, plump turnovers, these half-moon ravioli were nourishing as well as satisfying. My brother and I not only happily consumed them each week, we also participated in their creation. After my mother rolled out the dough, spooned on the filling, and tightened the stuffed centers, she called us into the kitchen. Our job was to seal the ravioli closed by pinching their edges together with the tines of a fork.

Today I pick up my fork where I left it off in childhood, shaping my macaroni with variety. I, who never saw even ricotta inside a noodle, now make orange raviolini with a fruit and nut filling, black pepper crabmeat agnolotti, sun-dried tomato tortelloni stuffed with goat cheese, and much, much more for customers, friends, and family. Everywhere, regional distinctions have been blurred. In fact, the only limits to the shape and substance of filled macaroni these days are a cook's own imagination. That's why in this chapter I've given instructions on how to form basic macaroni shapes first; the recipes for the fillings follow separately, starting on page 56. How to mix and match the form with the filling, not to mention what flavor to choose for the dough and what sauce should top the dish, is entirely up to you.

I do, however, have two recommendations for you to remember when making filled macaroni. First, always double the basic macaroni dough recipe (see pages 23–25) to serve four to six people. After briefly kneading it, divide your lump of dough in half so you can roll out two pieces of the right size and

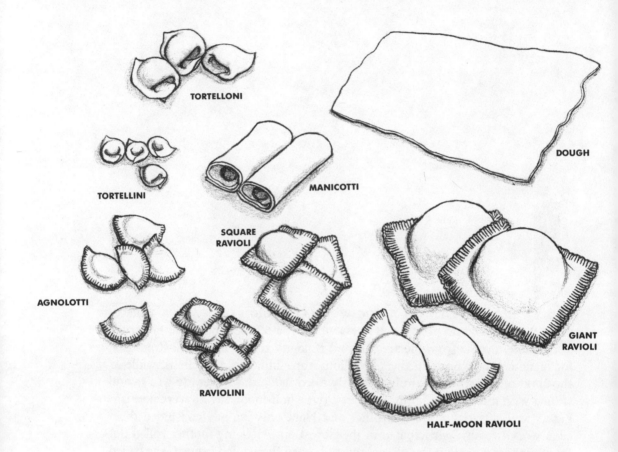

TORTELLONI

DOUGH

TORTELLINI

MANICOTTI

SQUARE RAVIOLI

AGNOLOTTI

GIANT RAVIOLI

RAVIOLINI

HALF-MOON RAVIOLI

thickness. The second is always to try to prepare your filling before your macaroni, because dough that sits out too long loses its pliability. If you feel your dough drying as you work with it, let it rest under a towel, or anything else large enough to cover it, for about ten minutes. At least some of the dough's original elasticity should return. (For more information on making homemade macaroni, see the previous chapter.)

The instructions below begin after you have rolled out your doubled dough recipe into two rough circles or ovals, each the thickness of a nickel and measuring about twenty-three inches in diameter. In other words, let's start just before my mother would call my brother and me into the kitchen. ◆

HALF-MOON RAVIOLI

1. Lay your rolled-out circles or ovals of dough on the work surface in front of you. Place a heaping tablespoon of filling 1 inch from the edge of the dough.

Place a tablespoon of filling about 1 inch from the corner of the dough.

2. Fold the edge of the dough over the lump of filling, forming a half-moon approximately 4 inches across and 3 inches wide.

3. Using the edges of your fingers, shape the macaroni around the filling. Then cut along the perimeter of the half-moon with a sharp knife.

Fold the dough over the filling and use your fingers to form the half-moon shape.

4. Seal the edges of the ravioli closed, first with your fingertips, then with the tines of a fork.

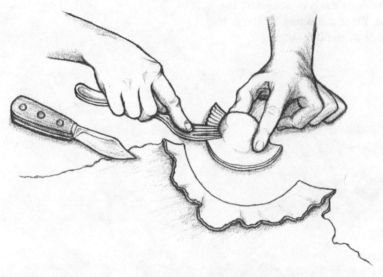

After you have cut around the perimeter of the ravioli, use the tines of a fork to crimp and seal the edges together.

5. Repeat until you have used up all the dough. If necessary, roll together the remnant pieces of dough to form a new, smaller circle or oval. And if you have any pieces left over, you can cook them along with the ravioli. You can refrigerate the ravioli for a few hours before cooking, or freeze for a longer period.

6. Bring at least 6 quarts of water to a boil. Drop in the ravioli, one at a time. When the water returns to a boil, cook for 10 minutes, resubmerging with a big spoon any ravioli that surface. Drain in a colander.

SQUARE RAVIOLI

1. Cut your rolled-out dough into rectangles measuring about 5 × 10 inches.

2. Lay a rectangular sheet of dough on the work surface in front of you. Place a heaping teaspoon of filling at regular intervals along the length of the sheet. You should fit eight heaping teaspoons along this bottom sheet.

3. Lay another rectangular sheet over the first. Using the flat of your hand, tighten the dough around each lump of filling, forming squares.

4. With a sharp knife, cut along the edges of the squares to produce the ravioli.

5. Seal the edges of the ravioli closed, first with your fingertips, then with the tines of a fork.

6. Repeat the procedure with the other rectangular sheets. Cut whatever small pieces of dough are left into long or short strands and cook along with the ravioli.

7. Bring at least 6 quarts of water to a boil. Drop in the ravioli, one at a time. When the water returns to a boil, cook for 10 minutes, resubmerging with a big spoon any ravioli that surface. Drain in a colander.

RAVIOLINI

Follow the same procedure as for square ravioli, placing just 1/4 teaspoon of filling along the length of a rectangular sheet to make raviolini. This method is the easiest way to make raviolini. However, if you'd like, you can purchase a raviolatrici, an inexpensive ravioli tray that looks like a metal ice tray with serrated edges and 36 separate compartments. To be honest, I've never been able to get mine to come out right using the tray. But if you are using one, proceed as follows:

1. Cut your rolled-out dough into rectangles slightly larger than your ravioli tray.

2. Lay a rectangular sheet of dough across the tray. Trim the dough to fit the tray, leaving about 1/2 inch of dough dangling over the edges. Press the dough into the tray's individual compartments.

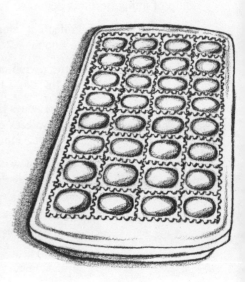

3. Place 1/4–1/2 teaspoon of filling into each compartment. Lay another rectangular sheet of dough across the top of the tray.

4. With a rolling pin, roll across the top of the tray to seal the serrated edges of the individual compartments. Continue to roll until the excess dough pulls away from the tray and the raviolini are formed.

5. Separate the raviolini from the tray by turning the tray upside down. If the individual raviolini are still joined and won't release from the tray, use a knife to trim around the edges of the individual compartments. If the edges of the ravioli are not quite closed after their release, use the tines of a fork to tighten the seals.

6. Repeat the procedure with the other rectangular sheets.

7. Bring at least 6 quarts of water to a boil. Drop in the raviolini, one at a time. When the water returns to a boil, cook 7–8 minutes, resubmerging with a big spoon any raviolini that surface. Drain in a colander.

AGNOLOTTI

1. Follow the same procedure as for half-moon ravioli, placing just ¼ teaspoon of filling ½ inch in from the edge of the dough to form 1-inch agnolotti.

2. To cook, bring at least 6 quarts of water to a boil. Drop in the agnolotti and stir. When the water returns to a boil, cook 7–8 minutes, resubmerging with a big spoon any agnolotti that surface. Drain in a colander.

GIANT RAVIOLI

1. Cut your rolled-out dough into rectangles measuring about 5 × 10 inches.

2. Lay a rectangular sheet on the work surface in front of you. Place ½ cup of filling about 2 inches in from one edge of the rectangle and another ½ cup of filling about 2 inches in from the other edge.

3. Lay another rectangular sheet over the first. Using the flat of your hand, tighten the dough around both lumps of filling, forming two squares.

4. With a sharp knife, cut along the edges of the squares to produce two giant ravioli.

5. Seal the edges of the ravioli closed, first with your fingertips, then with the tines of a fork. (You can trim the edges to make perfectly even squares.)

6. Repeat the procedure to produce 8 giant ravioli.

7. Bring at least 10 quarts of water to a boil. Drop in the giant ravioli one at a time. When the water returns to a boil, cook for 15 minutes, resubmerging with a big spoon any ravioli that surface. Drain in a colander.

TORTELLINI (CAPPELLETTI)

1. Cut your rolled-out circles or ovals of dough into 1 × 1-inch squares.

2. Place one square on the work surface in front of you and angle it in the shape of a diamond. Dab a pea-sized amount of filling in the middle of the diamond.

To make tortellini, place a pea-sized dot of filling on a 1-inch square of dough.

Fold the dough in half to form a triangle, bring the two base corners of the triangle together, and pinch to seal.

3. Fold over one corner of the diamond to the opposite corner to form a triangle. Using your fingertips, seal the edges of the triangle by pressing them together.

4. Take the two base corners of the triangle and fold them together over your thumb. With your index finger, pinch the seal together, forming the shape of a little peaked hat.

5. Repeat the procedure with each square of dough.

6. Bring at least 6 quarts of water to a boil. Drop in the tortellini and stir. When the water returns to a boil, cook 7–8 minutes, resubmerging with a big spoon any tortellini that surface. Drain in a colander.

TORTELLONI

Follow the same procedure as for tortellini, forming 2 × 2-inch squares for tortelloni. Dab ½ teaspoon filling inside each tortelloni diamond.
Cook the same way as tortellini.

MANICOTTI

1. Cut your rolled dough into rectangles measuring about 5 × 10 inches.

2. Lay a rectangular sheet on your work surface with the short edge facing you. Place ⅓ cup filling close to the edge nearest you. Using your fingers, form the filling into a narrow strip running from one side of the rectangle to the other.

3. Roll the dough over the filling twice, in jelly-roll fashion. Trim off the excess dough to complete the first manicotti.

4. Repeat the procedure with the remainder of the first rectangular sheet and with the other sheets. Each rectangle should yield three manicotti.

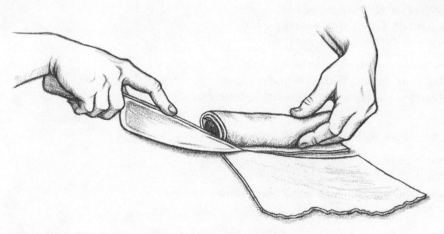

After the manicotti is rolled, trim off the excess dough.

5. Cover the bottom of a shallow oblong pan or casserole dish with sauce. Place the manicotti in the dish, 1 inch apart. Cover the manicotti generously with more sauce. Sprinkle the top with grated Parmesan or Romano, or with shredded mozzarella or fontina, or with any favorite cheese of yours. Bake, covered, in a 400-degree oven for 30 minutes. Uncover and bake for an additional 15 minutes.

MEAT FILLING

Serves 4–6

This is the only filling I ever ate as a child. It's simple but versatile and we never tired of it. Neither will you.

1. Using your hand or a fork, combine all the ingredients thoroughly. The filling will be soft and moist.

2. Roll out your dough in whatever shape you'd like and fill.

1 pound lean ground beef

3 eggs

1 cup coarsely grated Romano cheese

1/2 cup coarsely chopped fresh Italian parsley

MODENESE FILLING

Rosie, our Italian cook at the store, shared this recipe from her hometown of Modena. There, she says, people like to shape tortellini with this tasty meat and cheese filling and cook it in soup. I tried the filling in a handmade ravioli, topped with just a little butter and cheese, and loved it.

1. Place chicken in a pot and cover with water. Bring to a boil, reduce heat, and simmer for 10 minutes. Remove from heat. In a food processor fitted with the steel blade, chop chicken until fairly fine. Reserve.

2. Melt the butter and heat the oil and butter together in a skillet over medium high heat. Add the onions and sauté. After about 5 minutes, when the onions are beginning to wilt, add the salami. Mix well. Cook 2–3 minutes more. Add the lean ground beef and brown.

3. When the ground beef is cooked through, stir in the reserved chicken. Add the salt, pepper, and grated nutmeg. Remove from heat.

4. When the filling has cooled, mix in the Parmesan and the beaten egg.

5. Roll out your dough in whatever shape you'd like, and fill.

1 pound boneless, skinned chicken breasts

4 tablespoons (1/2 stick) butter

3 tablespoons oil

1 yellow onion, peeled and coarsely chopped

1/4 pound thinly sliced salami, cut in small pieces

1 pound lean ground beef

1 teaspoon salt

1 teaspoon coarsely ground black pepper

1/2 whole nutmeg, grated

1 cup coarsely grated Parmesan cheese

1 egg, beaten

PESTO-RICOTTA FILLING

My fascination with fresh basil keeps me experimenting with this tricky little herb. Pesto-ricotta filling is one of my successful basil-inspired inventions.

1. Combine all the ingredients in a food processor fitted with the steel blade. Process until the mixture is thick and smooth.

2. Roll out your dough in whatever shape you'd like and fill.

1 pound ricotta cheese

2 eggs

1 cup pesto (see page 75)

1 cup coarsely grated Romano cheese

1 teaspoon coarsely ground black pepper

SPINACH-PROSCIUTTO FILLING

Serves 4–6

My husband, Cosmo, gets at least partial credit for this one. He was the one who suggested doing a spinach filling in the first place. I'm a little reluctant to give him all the credit because in all seriousness, this filling is about the best there is.

1. Combine the spinach, eggs, and black pepper in a food processor fitted with the steel blade. Process until finely chopped and transfer to a bowl.

2. Chop the prosciutto until fine in the food processor. Add to the bowl.

3. Using your hands, mix in the Romano.

4. Roll out your dough in whatever shape you'd like, and fill.

2 10-ounce packages frozen spinach, thawed, or 3 cups cooked fresh spinach

2 eggs

1 tablespoon coarsely ground black pepper

1/2 pound prosciutto, sliced

1 1/2 cups coarsely grated Romano cheese

PARSLEY FILLING

Serves 4–6

This filling is more flavorful and more nutritious than you might expect. That's because parsley is rich in vitamins A and C. Use only the fresh flat Italian variety for this recipe, please.

1. In a food processor fitted with a steel blade, chop 2 bunches of the parsley until fine. Add 2 of the eggs and the other 2 bunches of parsley and process again until the mixture is smooth. Transfer to a bowl.

2. Beat the other 2 eggs. Combine the beaten eggs, pepper, salt, and Parmesan with the parsley mixture in the bowl.

3. Roll out your dough in whatever shape you'd like and fill.

4 bunches Italian parsley

4 eggs

1 heaping teaspoon coarsely ground black pepper

1/2 teaspoon salt

3 cups coarsely grated Parmesan cheese

GOAT CHEESE FILLING

I was never a lover of goat cheese until I met dozens of people who were. Their raves about the little logs shot through with herbs or covered with ash sparked my interest and culinary curiosity. Not only did I acquire a taste for the cheese but to my surprise, I also found that I enjoyed cooking with it. Nowadays Cremaldi's customers hear me singing the praises of fresh goat's milk cheeses. Needless to say, I also love this filling.

1. Combine all of the ingredients in a food processor fitted with the steel blade. Process until mixture is thick and smooth.

2. Roll out your dough in whatever shape you'd like and fill.

3/4 pound goat cheese
1 pound ricotta cheese
1 tablespoon dried basil
1 egg
2 cups plain bread crumbs
1/2 teaspoon salt

Serves 4–6

Fortunately, Gorgonzola doesn't taste the way it smells. When I was a child and watched my grandmother spread the cheese on hot bread, the strong odor would make me turn away. I've long since overcome my childhood aversion. In fact, this filling has exactly the opposite effect on me and just about everyone else.

1. Combine the Gorgonzola, bread crumbs, ricotta, eggs, and black pepper in a food processor fitted with the steel blade. Process until smooth and transfer to a bowl.

2. Using your hands, mix in the grated Parmesan.

3. Roll out your dough in whatever shape you'd like, and fill.

3/4 pound Gorgonzola cheese or another blue-veined cheese
1 cup plain bread crumbs
1 1/2 cups ricotta cheese
2 eggs
1 teaspoon coarsely ground black pepper
1 1/2 cups coarsely grated Parmesan cheese

LOBSTER FILLING

I thought about this filling for weeks before I actually made it, and then I couldn't believe how good it tasted. You can savor its delicate flavors in ravioli bathed in a light tomato sauce or dotted with just a little butter and black pepper. But however you serve this delicious filling, don't wait as long as I did to try it.

1. Peel the lemon. Process the lemon peel until very fine in a food processor fitted with the steel blade.

2. Add the Ritz crackers and the basil leaves to the lemon peel and process together until very fine. Transfer the mixture to a bowl.

3. Place the lobster meat in the processor and process briefly so that it isn't too fine.

4. Melt the stick of butter and pour it over the lemon peel, cracker, and basil mixture. Add the lobster meat. Squeeze the juice of the lemon over the mixture. With a spoon, combine all of the ingredients in the bowl until they are well incorporated.

5. Roll out your dough in whatever shape you'd like and fill.

1 lemon

36 (1 stack pack) Ritz crackers

1 cup fresh basil leaves

1/2 pound cooked lobster meat (fresh or frozen)

8 tablespoons (1 stick) butter

CRABMEAT FILLING

Your guests will never suspect that this elegant filling is so easy to make. Serve it in a graceful tortellini accented by a sophisticated sauce like Lemon Scallop and you will have created an impressive first course for an important dinner.

1. Using your hand or a fork, combine all the ingredients thoroughly.

2. Roll out your dough in whatever shape you'd like and fill.

6 ounces canned crabmeat

2 eggs

3/4 cup coarsely grated Parmesan cheese

1 heaping tablespoon chopped fresh or dried chives

2 tablespoons Marsala or sherry

SHRIMP FILLING

Serves 4–6

Use only fresh shrimp, if you can. You'll be glad you did.

1. Boil shrimp 5–7 minutes. Drain. In a food processor fitted with the steel blade, chop until fairly fine and set aside.

2. Melt the butter in a skillet over medium high heat. Add the shallots. Cook for 3 minutes. Add the shrimp and cook briefly until the shrimp are warmed through. Remove skillet from heat.

3. Mix in the chopped pecans, ricotta, Parmesan, and the beaten egg. Season with the salt and pepper.

4. Roll out your dough in whatever shape you'd like, and fill.

1 pound fresh medium shrimp, shelled and deveined, or frozen shrimp, thawed

4 tablespoons (1/2 stick) butter

3 shallots, chopped

1 cup pecans, coarsely chopped

1 heaping cup ricotta cheese

1 cup coarsely grated Parmesan cheese

1 egg, beaten

1 teaspoon salt

1 teaspoon coarsely ground black pepper

PORCINI FILLING

Serves 4–6

You'll like cooking this filling almost as much as you'll enjoy eating it in macaroni. As the porcini boil away, they release a powerful and irresistible aroma.

1. Boil the porcini in the 4 cups of water for 10 minutes. Drain.

2. In a food processor fitted with the steel blade, combine the porcini, ricotta, mozzarella, and eggs. Process until smooth and transfer to a bowl.

3. Add the Romano, black pepper, and garlic powder to the porcini mixture. Mix together thoroughly.

4. Roll out your dough in whatever shape you'd like and fill.

3 ounces dried porcini mushrooms

4 cups water

1 pound ricotta cheese

1/4 pound mozzarella cheese (whole milk or skim)

2 eggs

1 1/2 cups coarsely grated Romano cheese

1 teaspoon coarsely ground black pepper

1 teaspoon garlic powder

VEGETABLE FILLING

Serves 4–6

Perfecting this filling wasn't easy. Not that all the flavor combinations I came up with weren't good, but the texture never seemed quite right and, what was worse, the filling kept leaking out when I cooked the ravioli. But I stuck with it, and finally found a great vegetable filling that works.

1. Dice the carrots, celery, zucchini, and scallions. Mince the garlic.

2. Melt the butter in a large skillet over medium high heat. Add the minced vegetables along with the pepper and salt. Sauté the vegetables until they cook down.

3. After about 10 minutes, when the vegetables are slightly wilted, pour in the port. Continue to cook for 5 more minutes. Then remove the skillet from the heat and let the mixture cool.

4. Coarsely process the vegetable mixture in a food processor fitted with the steel blade. Transfer to a bowl.

5. Combine the bread crumbs and beaten eggs with the vegetables. Mix well.

6. Roll out your dough in whatever shape you'd like and fill.

2 large carrots, trimmed
2 stalks celery
1 pound zucchini
1 bunch scallions
4 garlic cloves, peeled
8 tablespoons (1 stick) butter
1 heaping teaspoon coarsely ground black pepper
1 1/2 teaspoons salt
1/2 cup port or sherry
2 cups plain bread crumbs
2 eggs, beaten

FRUIT AND NUT FILLING

Serves 4–6

I had always found few foods more festive than cookies or cakes with a fruit and nut filling. Now I think putting this great combination inside a ravioli may be more festive still, itself a reason to celebrate.

1. Place hazelnuts on a cookie sheet and set in a 425-degree oven for 20 minutes to toast. (If nuts are not already skinned, skin them yourself by rubbing them between your hands when they're just toasted and still hot.)

2. Meanwhile, place the apricots in a pot and cover with cold water. Boil them for 20 minutes until they get plump. Drain.

1 1/2 cups shelled hazelnuts, skinned, or skin them yourself after toasting
1 1/2 cups dried apricots
1 cup Cointreau liqueur
1 1/2 cups ricotta cheese
2 eggs, beaten

3. Place the apricots and Cointreau in a food processor fitted with the steel blade, and coarsely chop. Transfer to a bowl.

4. Finely chop the toasted hazelnuts in the food processor and combine them with the apricot mixture. Mix in the ricotta and beaten eggs.

5. Roll out your dough in whatever shape you'd like, and fill.

PUMPKIN FILLING

Serves 4–6

Mention a pumpkin filling and most people will think of a dessert. But this semi-sweet filling, in a ravioli, tortelloni, or any shape whatever, makes a surprisingly satisfying main course, especially when topped with our Famous Tomato Sauce.

1. Combine all of the ingredients in a large bowl. Mix well with a spoon or your hands.

2. Roll out your dough in whatever shape you'd like, and fill.

1 can (15 ounces) pumpkin or squash

1 pound ricotta cheese

1 heaping tablespoon nutmeg

1½ cups coarsely grated Parmesan cheese

1 teaspoon sugar

¼ pound (2 dozen) miniature macaroons (preferably Italian amaretti), ground to a powder

2 eggs, beaten

1 cup plain bread crumbs

IT TOOK MY MOTHER TEN YEARS TO CREATE TRIO'S FAMOUS RED Sauce. Figuratively speaking, the sauce began cooking the day her clear, full Abruzzi flavors met my father's strong Sicilian tastes over a hot stove. But as in any strong, enduring union, it took time and patience and a willingness to experiment to achieve a perfect blending of the two. The result was worth the wait. Just ask the airline pilots who fly gallons of it home to San Francisco, the Italians who say they've finally found a red sauce like the one their mothers used to make, and all the other customers who regularly line up to buy it.

Like all good things, the secret of the Famous Tomato Sauce recipe that follows is its simplicity. To this day, some people think that it takes hours to prepare or that it relies on a complex base of meat or fish. It's really much easier to make than that. In fact, it usually isn't hard to invent a sauce yourself if you have a love of food, the need, and a little imagination. My version of pesto was born during my early romance with basil. A quick tomato sauce was the result of unexpected company arriving for dinner one evening and my having nothing to serve them. And Lemon Scallop is just a new twist on an old favorite combination. Many of my sauces were originally intended to accompany a particular flavor of macaroni. Like Pesto and basil-flavored pasta or the more subtle sauce of prosciutto and cream over nutmeg, these sauces and macaroni have complementary tastes or share an important element. As my daughter Genevieve says, mixing and matching the two is a lot like putting together an outfit.

I do not, however, subscribe to any of those silly rules about which sauce to serve on what shape pasta. Why should you top your spaghetti with an Alfredo or some other cream sauce if you prefer to drench it in a hearty Bolognese? Or why should you trap meat or vegetables inside rigatoni, for instance, if you prefer to catch white clam or melted cheese? As in all matters of taste, be your own judge: the individual palate provides a better guide than any so-called expert's pronouncement.

You may even find yourself tempted to try the sauces in this chapter with more than just pasta, inventing your own settings, pairings, and accompaniments. With its haunting flavor, Parsley Sauce is an irresistible dip, for instance; veal and Pesto make a great sandwich; and Orange Sauce is an elegant baster for roast chicken. Sometimes my craving for a sauce can even become the compelling reason to make a particular dish.

No matter what the context, though, these sauces are always recognizable. Whether it is Porcini, Spinach-Nut, Broccoli Cream, or whatever, they taste like the ingredients in their titles. Like our Famous Tomato Sauce, their flavors are clear, strong, and unforgettable. Enjoy them. ◆

FAMOUS TOMATO SAUCE

Makes 3 quarts

This is quite simply, the best red sauce there is—similar to the one my parents have made and sold in their North End store for years. Freeze it so you can always have some available.

1. Chop the garlic until it is fine, either in a food processor fitted with the steel blade or by hand.

2. Heat the oil on high heat in a Dutch oven or large saucepan with at least a 5-quart capacity. Add the garlic and cook until light brown.

3. Stir in the tomatoes, juice, and tomato cans of water. Add the pepper, parsley, basil, sugar, and salt. Stir again.

4. When the sauce begins to boil, reduce the heat. Simmer, stirring occasionally, about 45 minutes.

1 head garlic (3/4 cup garlic cloves), peeled

3/4 cup oil

2 cans (1 pound, 12 ounces each) crushed peeled tomatoes, with juice

8 cups (2 tomato cans) water

1 teaspoon finely ground black pepper

1/2 teaspoon dried parsley

1 heaping teaspoon dried basil

1 heaping tablespoon plus 1 teaspoon sugar

2 heaping teaspoons salt

15-MINUTE TOMATO SAUCE

Makes enough sauce for 1–1½ pounds macaroni

The arrival of unexpected company one evening led to the creation of this fast, reliable tomato sauce. With its bite-size chunks of tomato, the sauce is beautiful to look at as it decorates the plainest of pastas. It can also become addictive.

1. Heat the oil in a large skillet over medium heat. Using a garlic press, add all 8 garlic cloves and cook until golden, about 3 minutes.

2. Add the tomatoes, breaking them up a little in the skillet. Raise the heat to high so that the sauce begins to bubble.

3. Stir in the sugar, basil, pepper, and salt. Then let the sauce bubble, uncovered, for another 10 minutes, continuing to stir occasionally.

1/4 cup oil

8 garlic cloves, peeled

15 ounces (1 can) peeled plum tomatoes

1 tablespoon sugar

1/2 teaspoon dried basil

1/2 teaspoon coarsely ground black pepper

1/2 teaspoon salt

REAL FAST MEAT SAUCE

Makes enough sauce for 1–1½ pounds macaroni

This sauce was originally an improvisation, put together with ingredients I always like to have close at hand.

1. Heat the oil in a large skillet over medium high heat. Add the garlic. Then add the lean ground beef, breaking it up with a spoon.

2. Sprinkle in the oregano, pepper, and salt. Stirring often, cook until the meat browns.

3. When the meat is browned, add the tomatoes, breaking them up slightly, and the sugar. Let the sauce simmer, uncovered, for 30 minutes, stirring occasionally.

1/4 cup oil

1 garlic clove, peeled and minced

1 pound lean ground beef

1/2 teaspoon dried oregano

1/2 teaspoon finely ground black pepper

1/2 teaspoon salt

1 pound, 12 ounces canned whole peeled tomatoes

1 tablespoon sugar

LO-CAL TOMATO SAUCE

Makes enough sauce for 1–1½ pounds macaroni

The glorious colors of this uncooked sauce will remind you of the pleasures of summer.

Combine all the ingredients in a food processor fitted with the steel blade. Process for about 15 seconds so that sauce is still slightly chunky.

4 large or 8 small tomatoes, quartered

2 cups fresh basil

1 large onion, peeled and quartered

2 large garlic cloves, peeled

1/2 teaspoon coarsely ground black pepper

1/2 teaspoon salt

2 tablespoons olive oil

GRANDMOTHER'S THREE-MEAT TOMATO SAUCE

Makes 4 quarts sauce

Actually, it wasn't my grandmother but my Aunt Honey, who lived with her and helped with all the cooking and canning, who taught me how to make this favorite family sauce. I guess I was around eight or nine when Honey showed me how to fry the meat, mix in the tomato paste, and add the vegetables. Honey always had such patience with me. And that was how my romance with cooking began.

1. Heat the oil in a Dutch oven over medium high heat. When the oil is hot, place the chicken parts, stewing beef, and sausage together in the Dutch oven and brown over high heat for 10 minutes, turning the meats often.

2. Reduce the heat slightly and continue to cook, as you turn the meats, for 20 more minutes.

3. Mix in the tomato paste, stirring it to coat all the meat. Then add the water, onion, carrot, and celery, along with the pepper, salt, and bay leaf. Reduce the heat to a simmer and cook the sauce for 1½ hours. Remove bay leaf.

4. Ladle the sauce over your noodles and serve the meat in a separate dish, chicken bones and all.

NOTE: My grandmother always used her tomato paste cans to measure the water for the sauce. But since they are 6-ounce cans, empty them into a measuring cup or quart jar to add up to the 4 quarts (or 16 cups) of water needed.

1/2 cup oil
Parts of a chicken—
    2 drumsticks
    2 wings
    2 thighs
1/2 pound stewing beef, cut in pieces
3/4 pound (4 links) sweet Italian sausage
24 ounces (4 cans) tomato paste
4 quarts water (see Note)
1 whole medium onion, peeled
1 carrot, scraped and cut in half
1 celery stalk with leaves, cut in half
1 teaspoon coarsely ground black pepper
1 tablespoon salt
1 bay leaf

GAETA SAUCE

Just north of Naples, along Italy's Tyrrhenian seacoast, is the town of Gaeta where my husband Cosmo's family is from and where the famous olives are grown. (Gaeta black olives are similar to Greek olives and are packed in brine.) It seems appropriate that I first tasted this memorable olive sauce in another Cremaldi home by the sea, with Cosmo's Aunt Mary and Uncle Angelo Tuccelli on Martha's Vineyard.

1. Heat the oil in a skillet over medium high heat. Add the onions, garlic, and olives, and season with the red pepper, oregano, black pepper, and salt. Cook until the onions are lightly browned.

2. When the onions are cooked, mix in the tomato paste, stirring continuously. Add the tomatoes, breaking them up with a spoon. Pour in the 1/2 cup water and lower the heat. Simmer for 15 minutes.

1/4 cup oil

1 yellow onion, peeled and sliced

4 large garlic cloves, peeled and minced

1 1/2 cups pitted whole Gaeta olives

1 teaspoon crushed red pepper

1/2 teaspoon oregano

1/2 teaspoon coarsely ground black pepper

1/2 teaspoon salt

12 ounces (2 small cans) tomato paste

2 pounds, 3 ounces canned whole peeled Italian tomatoes, with juice

1/2 cup water

BOLOGNESE SAUCE

Makes enough sauce for 1½ pounds macaroni

Ask most Americans to imagine a meat sauce and they'll picture a Bolognese. Italians call Bolognese a ragù, a term derived from a French verb meaning "to arouse taste." That arousal starts when you fry a mixture of carrots, celery, and onion called a battuto, to which you add garlic, meat, and tomatoes. Many Italian cooks still believe a good ragù must simmer for at least three hours. We prepare our Bolognese in much less time than that. It's just one of the reasons we think ours may be the best ragù around.

1. Heat the oil in a saucepan over medium high heat. Place the garlic, pancetta, carrots, celery, and onions in the hot oil and cook for 10 minutes.

2. When the vegetables are soft, add the ground beef, breaking it up in the saucepan. Cook until the color in the meat disappears.

3. Add the crushed and the whole tomatoes. Sprinkle in the pepper and salt. Add the bay leaves. Then let the sauce simmer for 1 hour, stirring occasionally.

4. Remove the sauce from the heat, take out the bay leaves, mix in the peas, and serve.

2 tablespoons oil

3 garlic cloves, peeled and minced

3 thin slices pancetta (Italian bacon)

2 medium carrots, scraped and sliced into ½-inch pieces

3 center ribs of celery, including leaves, sliced into ½-inch pieces

1 medium onion, peeled and sliced

1 pound extra lean ground beef

1 pound 12 ounces canned crushed tomatoes, with juice

2 pounds, 3 ounces canned whole peeled Italian tomatoes, with juice

1 teaspoon coarsely ground black pepper

1 teaspoon salt

2 bay leaves

1 cup frozen peas, thawed, or fresh peas, shelled

TOMATO-VEGETABLE SAUCE

Makes enough sauce for 1½ pounds macaroni

Like many classic French sauces, this one begins with a colorful medley of celery, carrots, and onions. And it's so easy to prepare, it just might become a classic in your repertoire too. Serve it over Manicotti Bolognese (see page 93) for a harmony of good tastes.

1. Place the celery, carrots, and onions in a food processor fitted with the steel blade. Process until the vegetables are chopped fine.

2. Heat the oil and melt the butter together in a skillet over high heat. Mix in the processed vegetables and the bay leaf and sauté for 5 minutes, stirring occasionally.

3. Add the tomatoes, breaking them up in the skillet. Lower the heat to medium high. Sprinkle in the pepper, salt, and sugar. Cook the sauce for 15 minutes. Remove bay leaf before serving.

1 celery stalk, quartered

1 carrot, scraped and quartered

1 onion, peeled and quartered

⅓ cup oil

4 tablespoons (½ stick) butter

1 bay leaf, broken in half

2 pounds, 3 ounces canned Italian peeled tomatoes, with juice

¼ teaspoon coarsely ground black pepper

1 teaspoon salt

1 teaspoon sugar

PARSLEY SAUCE

Makes enough sauce for 1–1½ pounds pasta

Once you taste this intriguing and powerful sauce, you won't be able to stop craving it. Just a dollop on your plate works wonders on any meat, salad, or cut vegetables. And on macaroni, parsley sauce is absolutely unforgettable. The recipe comes from my Italian neighbor and friend, Lena.

Combine all the ingredients in a food processor fitted with the steel blade. Process for about 15 seconds or until it becomes a thick, smooth sauce. (If you'd like a runnier sauce, you can add more oil by the tablespoon.)

4 cups Italian parsley, including tender part of stems

6 anchovy fillets

3 large garlic cloves, peeled

⅓ cup oil

1 tablespoon red wine vinegar

½ teaspoon crushed red pepper

PESTO

Makes enough sauce for 1–1½ pounds macaroni

Pesto, the glorious gourmet sauce originating in Genoa, Italy, is one of the joys of summer. Pure and simple, pesto requires only fresh basil to flavor it. It must be made during July and August when fresh basil is available, and then the sauce can be frozen and enjoyed year-round.

1. In a food processor fitted with the steel blade, combine the basil leaves, oil, garlic, and ¼ cup pine nuts. Process for 15 seconds and transfer to a bowl.

2. With a spoon, mix in the remaining pine nuts, left whole, along with the cheeses and black pepper.

2 cups fresh basil leaves, including the tender part of the stems, loosely packed in measuring cup

1 cup oil

5 large garlic cloves, peeled

½ cup pine nuts

¼ cup coarsely grated Parmesan cheese

¼ cup coarsely grated Romano cheese

½ teaspoon coarsely ground black pepper

SPINACH-NUT SAUCE

Makes enough sauce for 1–1½ pounds macaroni

Smooth and crunchy Spinach-Nut was the first sauce I ever invented. It was a hit back then in my parents' store, and judging by how much Cremaldi's customers enjoy it now, probably always will be.

1. Place the walnuts and the pecans in a food processor fitted with the steel blade. Process for about 5 seconds or until the nuts are coarsely chopped. Transfer the chopped nuts to a mixing bowl.

2. Place the spinach, oil, and garlic in the food processor. Sprinkle in the pepper and salt. Process until the mixture is very fine and then transfer to the same bowl as the nuts.

3. Add the slivered almonds to the bowl. With a spoon, mix until all of the ingredients are well incorporated. Serve over hot macaroni.

½ cup walnuts

½ cup pecans

10 ounces (1 package) fresh spinach, washed

¾ cup oil

6 garlic cloves, peeled

1 teaspoon coarsely ground black pepper

1 teaspoon salt

½ cup slivered almonds

BUTTER AND CREAM

Makes enough sauce for 1–1½ pounds macaroni

This simple—but rich—sauce complements any macaroni that has a subtle flavor. Reducing it slightly makes it thick enough to coat pasta of any shape.

Melt the butter in a skillet or small saucepan. Add the cream and cook on medium heat 10–15 minutes to reduce slightly, stirring often.

8 tablespoons (1 stick) butter
½ pint heavy cream

SESAME BUTTER

Makes enough sauce for 1–1½ pounds macaroni

This is a delicate sauce that can be made quickly and easily for an improvised dinner for two to twenty. Especially good over whole wheat pasta.

Melt the butter in a skillet. Add the sesame seeds, and with the heat on a medium high setting, cook, stirring, for five minutes, just long enough to brown the seeds slightly.

16 tablespoons (2 sticks) butter
⅓ cup sesame seeds

ALFREDO SAUCE

Makes enough sauce for 1–1½ pounds macaroni

This version of the Roman classic has become a bestseller at the store. Indulge yourself with this sauce on just about any macaroni, and it will taste the way you've always imagined Alfredo could be.

1. Melt the butter in a saucepan and then remove it from the heat.

2. Gradually whisk in the cream, ricotta, and black pepper. When these ingredients are well incorporated, whisk in the Romano, Parmesan, and fresh parsley.

8 tablespoons (1 stick) butter
½ pint heavy cream
¼ cup ricotta cheese
1 heaping teaspoon coarsely ground black pepper
¼ cup coarsely grated Romano cheese
½ cup coarsely grated Parmesan cheese
½ cup coarsely chopped Italian parsley

CRÈME FRAÎCHE SAUCE

Makes enough sauce for 1–1½ pounds macaroni

In the early sixties, a professor at the Massachusetts Institute of Technology, then still a student, was walking through Italy. Of all the sauces he tasted, and even savored, during his travels this was the one he has always remembered best. The professor, now a Cremaldi's customer, was kind enough to share the recipe with me.

Combine all the ingredients in a large bowl. Serve the sauce over cheese tortellini or other hot macaroni.

VARIATION: Add 1 large garlic clove, finely minced.

1 cup *Crème Fraîche (see below)*

3 *heaping tablespoons fresh basil, coarsely chopped*

½ *cup coarsely grated Parmesan cheese*

In a large mixing bowl, blend the heavy cream and the sour cream with a whisk. Cover loosely with plastic wrap and let stand at room temperature for at least 8 hours or until the Crème Fraîche begins to thicken and its tart flavor starts to develop. Cover and refrigerate until ready to use. (Crème Fraîche will keep in the refrigerator for several weeks.)

CRÈME FRAÎCHE

½ *cup heavy cream (not ultra-pasteurized)*

½ *cup sour cream*

BROCCOLI CREAM SAUCE

Makes enough sauce for 1–1½ pounds macaroni

What better way to serve this nourishing vegetable to kids who hate broccoli but love anything with macaroni? Of course, any adult would appreciate this sauce too.

Combine all the ingredients in a food processor fitted with the steel blade. Process for about 15 seconds or until it becomes a thick, smooth sauce. (If you like to keep the broccoli chunky, then process for only about 10 seconds.) Serve over hot macaroni.

1 *(10-ounce) package frozen broccoli, thawed, or 10 ounces fresh broccoli blanched*

½ *teaspoon salt*

½ *teaspoon finely ground white pepper*

½ *teaspoon nutmeg*

2 *garlic cloves, peeled*

1 *cup heavy cream*

PROSCIUTTO CREAM SAUCE

Makes enough sauce for 1–1½ pounds macaroni

Because I love the flavors of prosciutto and nutmeg, I could taste this sauce before I ever invented it. Actually eating it, especially over cheese tortelloni, was even better than I had imagined.

1. Pour the cream into a saucepan and reduce by boiling over low heat for 15 minutes.

2. Meanwhile, melt the butter in a skillet over medium high heat. Place the julienned prosciutto in the skillet and sauté for a few minutes. Then remove from heat.

3. When the cream is reduced, stir in the sautéed prosciutto along with the nutmeg. Mix well. Serve over any macaroni.

2 cups heavy cream
2 tablespoons butter
1/4 pound thinly sliced prosciutto, julienned
1 teaspoon nutmeg

CHERRY TOMATO CREAM SAUCE

Makes enough sauce for 1–1½ pounds macaroni

Everyone should have a recipe for a light, dressy sauce like this one. I like to serve Cherry Tomato Cream over rigatoni because of the way it gracefully seeps into the bends, twirls, and crevices.

1. Cut each cherry tomato in half.

2. Melt the butter in a skillet over medium high heat. When the butter is melted, pour in the oil. Add the halved tomatoes, along with the crushed red pepper and the dill weed. Raise the heat to high and sauté for 5 minutes.

3. Continuing to sauté, pour in the vodka and sprinkle in the salt. Stir. Pour in the heavy cream and sprinkle in the sugar. Stir again. Simmer for another 5 minutes, until the sauce is slightly reduced in volume and the tomatoes are starting to separate from their skins.

1 pint cherry tomatoes
8 tablespoons (1 stick) butter
1/2 cup oil
1/2 teaspoon crushed red pepper
1 heaping teaspoon dried dill weed
4 tablespoons vodka
1/4 teaspoon salt
1 cup heavy cream
1/4 teaspoon sugar

SAUCE FOR STRAW AND HAY

Makes enough sauce for 1–1½ pounds macaroni

The beauty of combining egg noodles (straw) and spinach noodles (hay) in one dish is its simplicity. This uncomplicated, yet sophisticated sauce, similar to an Alfredo, adds to Straw and Hay's great appeal. If you'd like, you can substitute asparagus tips or any vegetable you'd like for the peas.

1. Melt the butter in a large skillet. Add the prosciutto and sauté for about a minute. Stir in the cream and remove the sauce from heat.

2. Mix in the cheese and the peas. Serve over a combination of spinach pasta and egg pasta for color and flavor contrast.

16 tablespoons (2 sticks) butter

½ pound thinly sliced prosciutto, julienned

1 pint heavy cream

1 cup coarsely grated Parmesan cheese

1 package (8 ounces) frozen peas, thawed

GORGONZOLA SAUCE

Makes enough sauce for 1–1½ pounds macaroni

Italy's most famous blue-veined cheese is not for the faint of heart. Gorgonzola is strong in odor, creamy in texture, pungent in flavor and, for many people, absolutely irresistible. You won't be the first to succumb to this sauce.

1. Melt the butter in a saucepan over medium high heat. Add the sage to the melted butter and sauté for 1 minute.

2. Pour in the heavy cream and add the Gorgonzola to the saucepan. Lower the heat and stir the mixture continuously until the Gorgonzola is all melted. Keep the mixture from boiling.

3. Remove the saucepan from the heat. Mix in the grated Parmesan and Romano.

8 tablespoons (1 stick) butter

2 teaspoons dried sage leaves

2 cups heavy cream

¼ pound Gorgonzola cheese, broken into small pieces

1 cup coarsely grated Parmesan cheese

1 cup coarsely grated Romano cheese

WHITE CLAM SAUCE *Great* ♂♂

Makes enough sauce for 1–1½ pounds macaroni

Some people seem to think only the French can make a sauce without lumps. The French secret, of course, is constantly stirring the butter and flour to make the roux. Whisk the mixture here just as diligently as a French cook would and you'll get a White Clam Sauce that is as smooth as can be.

1. Melt the butter in a saucepan over medium high heat. Add the minced garlic and sauté for 3 or 4 minutes.

2. Add the flour, 1 tablespoon at a time, whisking constantly with the butter until together they form a roux. Lower the heat and simmer the roux for 5 minutes.

3. Slowly pour in the clam juice, whisking continuously to make sure the sauce is smooth.

4. Add the can of baby clams, including the liquid, then sprinkle in the pepper and thyme. Let the sauce simmer for 10 minutes.

5. Remove the sauce from the heat, add the chopped parsley, and serve.

8 tablespoons (1 stick) butter
6 large garlic cloves, peeled and minced
3 tablespoons flour
1 cup clam juice
1 can (10 ounces) whole baby + juice *clams,* ~~or~~ *10 ounces fresh clams,* ~~minced~~ cooked first - 6 pe pers
½ teaspoon coarsely ground black pepper
1 teaspoon thyme
1 cup coarsely chopped Italian parsley

LEMON SCALLOP SAUCE

Makes enough sauce for 1–1½ pounds macaroni

The scallops accent the zest in a refreshing reversal of the usual seafood and lemon combination. If you can find them, tiny, tender bay scallops are best for this lively and appealing sauce. Otherwise use whatever scallops, fresh or frozen, are available.

1. Grate the peel of the lemon.

2. Place the scallops in a mixing bowl. Squeeze the peeled lemon over the scallops to get all the juice and set the bowl aside.

3. Mince the shallot.

4. Melt 4 tablespoons of the butter in a saucepan over medium high heat, add the minced shallot, and sauté.

5. When the shallots turn golden brown and the butter

1 whole lemon
1 pound bay scallops
1 large shallot
6 tablespoons (¾ stick) butter
½ cup dry white wine
14 ounces canned peeled plum tomatoes
1 cup clam juice
1 teaspoon whole fennel seed

becomes hot and foamy, pour in the wine. Simmer for 1 minute, stirring.

6. Add the tomatoes, loosely breaking them up with a spoon. Simmer for 3 more minutes.

7. Stir in the clam juice, fennel seed, and black pepper. Reduce the heat to a low simmer.

8. Melt the remaining 2 tablespoons of butter in a separate skillet. Drain the scallops and sauté them in the skillet for 3 minutes, or until tender.

9. Combine the scallops and butter from the skillet with the sauce. Add the grated lemon peel and simmer, uncovered, over low heat for 20 minutes. Just before serving, sprinkle in the chopped parsley.

1/4 teaspoon coarsely ground black pepper

1/2 cup coarsely chopped Italian parsley

SMOKED SCALLOP SAUCE

Makes enough sauce for 1–1½ pounds macaroni

Purchasing smoked bay scallops can be a bit of an investment, but one that certainly pays off in flavor. This sauce tastes every bit as rich and classy as its main ingredient, found in specialty shops or supermarkets in cans or jars. The scallops just melt in your mouth.

1. Cut the scallops in quarters.

2. Melt the butter in a skillet over medium high heat. Add the scallops and sauté them for 3 minutes. Remove the cooked scallops from the skillet and reserve.

3. Sauté the scallions, red pepper, and garlic in the same skillet. Season with the salt and pepper.

4. Pour the heavy cream into the skillet. Cook the sauce, uncovered, for about 20 minutes, until the volume is reduced by half.

5. Just before serving, add the scallops to the sauce.

1 pound cold smoked bay scallops

8 tablespoons (1 stick) butter

1 bunch scallions, finely chopped

1 red bell pepper, cored, seeded, and minced

3 garlic cloves, peeled and minced

1/2 teaspoon salt

1 teaspoon finely ground black pepper

1 quart heavy cream

CALAMARI SAUCE

Makes enough sauce for 1 pound of macaroni

With its initial kick and subsequent tingle, the best word for this sauce is lively. Serve it over homemade lemon linguine with a good Chardonnay and be assured of stimulating anyone's palate.

1. Cut the squid bodies into half-inch rings. Slice the tentacles in half.

2. Melt the butter and heat the oil in a skillet over medium high heat. Add the chopped garlic, black pepper, and red pepper and sauté.

3. When the garlic is browned, add the calamari and pour in the lemon juice and clam juice. Reduce heat to a rapid simmer and cook the sauce for 5 minutes.

4. Remove the skillet from heat. Just before serving, stir in the parsley.

2 pounds cleaned fresh calamari (squid)

8 tablespoons (1 stick) butter

2/3 cup olive oil

1 whole head of garlic, peeled and chopped fine

1 teaspoon coarsely ground black pepper

1 teaspoon crushed red pepper

Juice of 1 lemon

1 cup clam juice

1 heaping cup coarsely chopped Italian parsley

TUNA SAUCE

Makes enough sauce for 1–1½ pounds macaroni

For me, this will always be a special sauce, rekindling memories of a special day. Like many Italian families, we ate only fish on Christmas Eve. And this tuna was the only red sauce my mother ever prepared for this holiday meal, serving it over spaghetti.

1. Heat the oil in a saucepan over medium high heat. Add the onion and fry until the slices are slightly cooked.

2. Add the tomato paste to the onions and cook for 3 minutes.

3. Mix the tuna into the tomato paste, stirring well. Then add the water, pepper, and sugar. Lower the heat and simmer the sauce for 10 minutes.

1/2 cup olive oil

1 small onion, peeled and sliced

12 ounces (2 cans) tomato paste

6½ ounces (1 can) Italian tuna packed in olive oil

2¼ cups (3 tomato paste cans) water

1 teaspoon white pepper

1 teaspoon sugar

SUN-DRIED TOMATO SAUCE

Makes enough sauce for 1–1½ pounds macaroni

The Italians have never found anything exceptional about sun-dried tomatoes—they just use them on a sandwich or as a garnish. But then we Americans got hold of these sweet and salty fruits, and made them out to be a sophisticated food. The only problem was that nobody knew what to do with them. This fabulous sauce offers one delicious solution.

1. Place the sun-dried tomatoes in a food processor fitted with the steel blade. (Don't worry if some of the oil the tomatoes are packed in ends up in the processor too.) Add the garlic, vegetable oil, ¼ cup of the pine nuts, and the black pepper. Process for 30 seconds and transfer to a bowl.

2. With a spoon, blend in the remaining pine nuts, left whole, along with the cheese and parsley. (If you prefer a runnier sauce, you can add up to another ¼ cup oil.)

- 20 *sun-dried tomatoes, packed in oil*
- 4 *large garlic cloves, peeled*
- ½ *cup vegetable oil or 10 percent olive oil*
- ½ *cup pine nuts*
- 1 *heaping teaspoon coarsely ground black pepper*
- ½ *cup coarsely grated Parmesan cheese*
- ½ *cup coarsely chopped Italian parsley*

ANCHOVY-PINE NUT-CURRANT SAUCE

Makes enough sauce for 1–1½ pounds macaroni

This is another authentic recipe that we were able to re-create thanks to one of my parents' North End customers. An elderly Italian woman described for me a flavorful sauce like this that she had often enjoyed in her youth. We'll never know if this re-creation quite matches the original, but my anchovy-pine nut-currant, especially when served over angel hair, is awfully good.

1. Melt the butter in a small skillet over medium high heat. Pour in the oil. Add the anchovies and mash them with a fork until they melt or begin to look like a paste.

2. When the anchovies are melted, stir in the pine nuts and currants. Cook the sauce for 2 more minutes.

- 8 *tablespoons (1 stick) butter*
- ½ *cup oil*
- 2 *ounces anchovies*
- ½ *cup pine nuts*
- ½ *cup dried currants*

GINGER-VERMOUTH SAUCE

Makes enough sauce for 1–1½ pounds macaroni

The intense aroma of sautéed gingerroot, when mixed with the other ingredients here, is indescribable. This versatile sauce is sensational not only on macaroni, but also on stir-fried chicken or fish.

1. Heat the oil in a saucepan over medium-high heat.

2. Meanwhile, in a food processor fitted with the steel blade, process the carrots, gingerroot, and garlic for 10 seconds each.

3. Add these ingredients, plus the sliced scallions, oregano, and red pepper, to the hot oil. Simmer uncovered for 5 minutes, stirring frequently.

4. Pour in the vermouth and simmer the sauce for 3 more minutes.

5. Add the water and salt. Simmer for 3 additional minutes.

1/2 cup oil

1 cup (about 2 medium) carrots, scraped and cut into 2-inch pieces

1/2 cup fresh gingerroot, peeled and cut into small pieces

4 garlic cloves, peeled

1 cup (about 8) scallions sliced in 1/4-inch pieces

1 heaping teaspoon dried oregano

1 heaping teaspoon crushed red pepper

1/2 cup vermouth

1/2 cup water

1/4 teaspoon salt

PORCINI SAUCE

Makes enough sauce for 1–1½ pounds macaroni

The powerful flavor of porcini mushrooms is concentrated in their limp brown bodies. Plump them up and mix them with brandy, beef broth, and the other ingredients here and their wild and wonderful mushroom taste is released. Whether you use it on macaroni or as a topping for steak, this terrific sauce may make you feel slightly wild too.

1. Boil the porcini in the water for 15 minutes to reconstitute. Remove from heat.

2. Melt the butter in a skillet over medium high heat. Add the shallots and fry until they are brown.

3. Drain the porcini (there probably won't be much water left) and add them to the melted butter and shallots. Raise the heat and cook together for 5 minutes.

2 cups (2½ ounces) dried porcini mushrooms

2 cups water

8 tablespoons (1 stick) butter

3 shallots, sliced

1 cup brandy

1½ cups beef broth

1/4 teaspoon white pepper

4. Add the brandy to the mixture in the skillet and simmer for 5 more minutes.

5. Pour in the beef broth. Sprinkle in the white pepper. Simmer the sauce for 10 additional minutes to blend the flavorings.

Makes enough sauce for 1–1½ pounds macaroni

This sauce is a charming and elegant accompaniment for orange or fruit-and-nut-filled macaroni, roast duck, or any other prepared poultry. If you're a little daring, pour the sauce right over a cooked bird.

1. Peel the orange and chop the peel until fine in a food processor fitted with the steel blade. Reserve the rest of the orange for its juice.

2. Melt the butter in a large skillet over medium high heat. Sauté the orange peel in the melted butter for about a minute.

3. Squeeze in the juice of the orange (it's nice if some of the pulp gets in too) along with the additional cup of orange juice. Simmer for about 15 minutes, until the volume is reduced by half.

4. Sprinkle in the cardamom. Stir. Pour in the cream. When the sauce returns to a low boil, cook for 2 more minutes, add the slivered almonds, and serve.

1 large orange
4 tablespoons (½ stick) butter
1 cup orange juice
1 tablespoon ground cardamom
½ pint heavy cream
½ cup slivered almonds

PASTA DISHES

LIKE OTHER ITALIAN-AMERICAN BABIES, I WASN'T FED BEECH-nut or Gerber's. My first real meal was a pasta dish, *pastina in brodo:* tiny bits of macaroni were cooked and then added to chicken broth where they floated. As older children we would enjoy fishing them out—*acini de pepe,* shaped like little dots, or miniature stars called *stellucce.* My mother knew back then that few meals are more nutritious or satisfying than pasta. As the runners who flock to her store each year the day before the Boston marathon say, "Eat pasta, run fasta!"

It was the Italians, of course, who first served pasta as a meal in itself, but we Americans should take credit for popularizing this one-dish approach. By the Civil War, macaroni baked with cheese and cream, a northern Italian specialty that the English had introduced to their colonies, was an affordable middle-class dinner. Several decades later, Americans were dining out in so-called "spaghetti joints" where they ordered a bottle of Chianti and a plate of spaghetti and meat balls. That dish, by the way, was invented here, probably when newly arrived Italian immigrants, never big meat eaters at home, discovered the cheaper and more plentiful American chopped beef.

Pasta dishes have been in style since then and probably always will be. Not the least important factor in pasta's appeal, I've always thought, is its versatility. My husband Cosmo grew up eating a different pasta meal five nights a week, ranging from Monday's *pasta e fagioli* to a fancy dish like manicotti or baked ziti on Sundays. At Cremaldi's, we cook at least three different kinds of lasagna regularly—red, white, and *al'orto* (garden vegetables). And the ingredients in the cold pasta salad we serve for lunch change daily. Our first prepared foods at the store were pasta dishes; they are still the staples of our business and our biggest sellers.

This chapter includes some familiar favorites and some new finds, along with two dishes which, although eaten as a first or a main course, aren't really pastas at all. One of these dishes, polenta, the cornmeal staple of northern Italy, is an ancient food first enjoyed by the Romans. The other dish, risotto, the medium-grain white rice that's cooked together with accompanying flavors, is currently the rage throughout Italy. With its wholesome ingredients, versatility, and thoroughly satisfying taste, who knows, one day risotto may become almost as popular as pasta. ◆

TRADITIONAL LASAGNA

Serves 4–6

Everybody has their own way of making a lasagna—this is ours. The sauce is what makes it so good. If you make this dish with homemade lasagna noodles, remember the noodles must be blanched and cooled before you're ready to start assembling the lasagna. (To blanch homemade lasagna noodles, immerse them in boiling water and remove them as soon as the water returns to a boil. Rinse the noodles in cold water.)

1. Cook the lasagna according to the package directions. Rinse in cold water, strain, and set aside.

2. Coarsely chop the mozzarella in a food processor fitted with the steel blade. Add the ricotta, 1 cup of the red sauce, the pepper, parsley, grated Romano, and eggs. Process until the mixture is thick and smooth. If necessary, add more sauce to make the mixture more spreadable.

3. Pour 1 cup of the red sauce across the bottom of a 9 × 13 × 2-inch baking pan. Arrange three lasagna strips, making sure they overlap a little, over the sauce. Spread 4 heaping tablespoons (or more if necessary) of the ricotta mixture over the lasagna and spread another cup of red sauce over that with the back of a spoon.

4. Repeat each layer, in the same order, four more times, ending with a layer of ricotta mixture and red sauce.

5. Sprinkle the Parmesan across the top of your lasagna. Bake at 400 degrees for 45 minutes to 1 hour, depending how firm you like it. For more firmness, cook longer and let set 15 minutes before slicing.

1 pound lasagna noodles

12 ounces mozzarella cheese, cut in small pieces

2 pounds ricotta cheese

1½ quarts Famous Tomato Sauce (see p. 00) or another homemade tomato sauce

1 teaspoon coarsely ground black pepper

¼ cup Italian parsley

1 cup coarsely grated Romano cheese

2 eggs

½ cup coarsely grated Parmesan cheese

VARIATION: Place slices of pepperoni, cooked sausage, or cooked hamburger on top of the ricotta layers. You can also add spinach, broccoli, cooked carrots, or any vegetable you like to the lasagna.

LASAGNA L'ORTO

Serves 4–6

This dish was born of necessity, or maybe I should say abundance—I invented it one day when we had too many vegetables at the store and nothing else to do with them. These days, making the popular lasagna l'orto has become the reason to buy the fresh vegetables featured in this nutritious and delicious dish.

1. Cube the eggplant. Slice the mushrooms. Slice the peppers. Cut the zucchini and the squash in a large dice. Slice the onion.

2. Mound all of the cut vegetables in a large Dutch oven or a pot. Pour the oil and sprinkle the black pepper and salt over the vegetables. Cook down over high heat until all of the vegetables are soft. Meanwhile, cook the lasagna noodles.

3. Cook the lasagna according to the package directions. Rinse in cold water, strain, and set aside.

4. When the vegetables have cooked down, stir in the tomatoes. Reduce heat to a simmer and cook for 10 minutes.

5. Spread 1½ cups of the vegetable mixture across the bottom of the baking pan. Place three strips of lasagna over the vegetables. Spread another 2 cups of the vegetable mixture over the lasagna. Then place eight slices of provolone over the vegetables.

6. Repeat the layers, ending with the remaining vegetables.

7. Sprinkle the Parmesan across the top of the lasagna. Bake in a 400-degree oven for 30 minutes until the cheese topping is melted and lightly browned.

VARIATION: For a spicier version of this lasagna, add 1 tablespoon of ground cumin to the vegetables as they cook.

1 *large eggplant*
2 *pounds mushrooms*
4 *green peppers* or *yellow or red*
2 *large zucchini*
1 *summer squash*
1 *large yellow onion (or 2 small onions), peeled*
1 *cup oil*
1 *heaping teaspoon coarsely ground black pepper*
1 *tablespoon salt*
1 *pound lasagna noodles*
1 *pound 12 ounces canned crushed tomatoes, with juice*
16 *slices provolone cheese*
1 *cup coarsely grated Parmesan cheese*

WHITE LASAGNA

Serves 8–10

This unusual and tantalizing lasagna from northern Italy blends the smooth innocence of béchamel (which the Italians call besciamella) with the seductiveness of pesto. The white sauce is set in between layers of pasta and fresh sliced tomatoes smothered in mozzarella. The dish is perfect for a first course or a light entrée.

BÉCHAMEL SAUCE

1 cup (2 sticks) butter

1 cup flour

6 cups milk

1 large onion, peeled and chopped

4 sprigs fresh Italian parsley, coarsely chopped

1 bay leaf, crumbled

1/2 teaspoon thyme

1/4 teaspoon finely ground black pepper

1/2 teaspoon nutmeg

1 teaspoon salt

3/4 cup Pesto Sauce (see p. 00)

1. Melt the butter in a saucepan over medium heat. Rapidly whisk in the flour, creating a paste, or roux. Cook the paste for 30 seconds, whisking continuously.

2. Continue to whisk while pouring all 6 cups of the milk into the saucepan in a steady stream.

3. Add the onions, parsley, and bay leaf. Season with the thyme, black pepper, nutmeg, and salt. Whisk the sauce again, vigorously, and let it simmer for 10 minutes to thicken, stirring often.

4. Remove the sauce from the heat. Fold in the Pesto and set aside until you're ready to assemble the lasagna.

LASAGNA

1 pound lasagna

All the Béchamel Sauce (see above)

5–6 fresh ripe tomatoes, sliced

1 1/2 pounds mozzarella cheese

1/2 cup bread crumbs

1/2 cup coarsely grated Romano cheese

1. Cook the lasagna according to the package directions. (You can always make your own lasagna noodles if you prefer, but packaged lasagna is more convenient and works just as well here.) Rinse, strain, and set aside.

2. Spread about a cup of the béchamel evenly across the bottom of a 9 × 13 × 2-inch baking pan. Arrange 4 lasagna sheets, making sure they overlap a little, over the béchamel. Spread another cup of the béchamel over the lasagna. Arrange a layer of tomatoes over the béchamel and a layer of mozzarella over the tomatoes. Spread more béchamel sauce over the mozzarella.

3. Repeat each layer, in the same order, three more times.

4. End with a layer of béchamel and top your lasagna with a mixture of the bread crumbs and Romano.

5. Bake the lasagna in a 400-degree oven for about 30 minutes, until the sauce is bubbling and the bread-crumb and cheese topping is melted and lightly browned.

MANICOTTI BOLOGNESE

Makes enough filling for 12 manicotti; serves 4–6

A mild red sauce will bring out the slight sharpness of the tasty filling from Bologna. If you don't want to cook them right away, the manicotti can be wrapped in aluminum foil and frozen. Remember to unwrap and thaw them before baking. If you forget to thaw them, these manicotti can still turn out nicely. Just bake them for 1 hour 15 minutes instead of 45 minutes, leaving them covered for half the time and uncovered for the second half. Either dried commercial or homemade manicotti works well for this dish. If you're using dried, boil the shells first and cut them open into rectangles to fill; if you're making your own manicotti shells, see pages 55–56 for instructions on how to shape them.

1. Place the onion in a food processor fitted with the steel blade. Process until fine and set aside. Process the salami until fine and set it aside. Do the same with the mozzarella.

2. Melt the butter in a skillet over medium high heat. Sauté the onions in the butter for 10 minutes.

3. Add the meat to the skillet, breaking it up with a spoon or fork. Cook until the meat is browned. Add the salami, black pepper, and nutmeg and cook together for 5 minutes.

4. Remove the mixture from the heat and let it cool.

5. Combine the bread crumbs, mozzarella, the 1 cup of Parmesan, and the beaten egg with the cooled mixture in the skillet. Incorporate thoroughly.

6. Place 1/3 cup of the incorporated filling mixture in the center of either a piece of dough cut for manicotti or a cooked, flattened manicotti shell. Form the filling into an oblong stretching across the dough or flattened shell. Then roll the manicotti.

7. Cover the bottom of a shallow baking dish with your favorite red sauce. Place the filled manicotti in the dish. Pour more of the red sauce over the manicotti, then sprinkle them with Parmesan. Bake, covered, in a 400-degree oven for 30 minutes. Uncover and bake for an additional 15 minutes.

1 medium onion, peeled

1/4 pound Genoa salami

1/4 pound mozzarella cheese

4 tablespoons (1/2 stick) butter

1 pound lean ground beef

1 teaspoon coarsely ground black pepper

1 teaspoon ground nutmeg

3/4 cup plain bread crumbs

1 cup grated Parmesan cheese, plus additional for sprinkling

1 egg, beaten

1 1/2 pounds homemade or commercial manicotti

2 quarts red sauce, preferably homemade

BAKED PENNE WITH PROSCIUTTO

Serves 4–6

Don't be afraid to substitute ziti, rigatoni, or your favorite tubular macaroni for the penne. It's the combination of flavors, rather than a particular pasta shape, that makes this dish so appealing.

1. Cook the pasta according to the package directions or until al dente.

2. Drain cooked pasta well and transfer to a large bowl. Pour 2 cups of the tomato sauce over the penne and mix well.

3. In a separate bowl, mix the ricotta, Romano, eggs, parsley, black pepper, prosciutto, Swiss cheese, and mozzarella with two more cups of the tomato sauce. Pour this mixture over the penne and mix well again, being careful not to break the pasta.

4. Transfer the pasta and sauce to a baking dish. Cover with the remaining 2 cups of sauce and sprinkle the top with a little more grated Romano. Bake in a 400-degree oven for 40 minutes or until the cheese is melted throughout.

1 pound penne or another tubular macaroni

6 cups Famous Tomato Sauce (see p. 69)

2 pounds ricotta cheese

1 cup coarsely grated Romano cheese, plus additional for sprinkling

2 eggs

4 tablespoons coarsely chopped Italian parsley

1 tablespoon coarsely ground black pepper

10 slices prosciutto, cut up small

6 slices Swiss cheese, cubed or chopped

6 slices or 12-ounce package mozzarella cheese, cut up small or shredded

RIGATONI AL FORNO

Al forno *means "from the oven." And Rosie, our Italian cook, surprised and delighted us one day when she pulled this traditional layered dish, dripping and oozing with cheese, out of our oven at the store. We've been surprising and delighting our customers with it ever since.*

1. Melt the butter and heat the oil in a large skillet over medium high heat. Add the onion slices and sauté until they turn a light brown.

2. Reduce the heat to medium. Add the ground beef, breaking it up with a spoon or fork. Season with the salt and pepper and cook until the meat is browned. Then remove skillet from the heat.

3. Mix in the Parmesan and 1 cup of the tomato sauce. Set aside.

4. Cook the rigatoni according to the package directions, adding a teaspoon of salt to the water. Drain well and transfer to a bowl. Then combine 1/2 cup of the meat mixture with the rigatoni.

5. Pour a cup of tomato sauce across the bottom of a baking pan or lasagna dish. Spoon half the rigatoni over the sauce. Cover the rigatoni with half the remaining meat mixture. Next, layer the cheeses: half the ricotta, followed by half the mozzarella slices, followed by a sprinkling of half the Romano.

6. Begin the second set of layers with the other half of the rigatoni, followed by the rest of the meat mixture, the rest of the ricotta, and the rest of the mozzarella. Top this by pouring on the last cup of tomato sauce and sprinkling on the rest of the Romano.

7. Bake the rigatoni in a 400-degree oven for 30 minutes.

8 tablespoons (1 stick) butter

2 tablespoons oil

1/2 yellow onion, peeled and sliced

3/4 pound lean ground beef

1/2 teaspoon salt

1/2 teaspoon coarsely ground black pepper

1 cup coarsely grated Parmesan cheese

3 cups Famous Tomato Sauce (see p. 69)

1 pound rigatoni

1 teaspoon salt

2 cups ricotta cheese

16 ounces mozzarella cheese, sliced

1/2 cup coarsely grated Romano cheese

JUMBO STUFFED SHELLS

Everyone I know, and even people I don't know, love these plumply stuffed shells that make a complete meal. I feel the same way.

1. Bring 5 quarts of water to a boil in a large pot. Drop in the shells and stir for the first few minutes until the water returns to a boil. Cover the pot with a lid and turn off the heat. Set a timer for 15 minutes.

2. After 15 minutes, place the shells under cold running water. When they are cold, drain them and reserve.

3. Place the ricotta, 1 cup of the Romano, and all the mozzarella, spinach, eggs, nutmeg, and black pepper in a bowl. Mix these filling ingredients with a spoon until they are well incorporated.

4. Pour 4 cups of your favorite tomato sauce across the bottom of a baking pan.

5. Stuff each shell with the filling. Set each stuffed shell in the baking dish.

6. Pour the other 4 cups of red sauce over the top of the shells. Sprinkle the remaining 1/2 cup of Romano over the sauce. Bake in a 400-degree oven for 45 minutes.

VARIATION: For a richer version of this dish, arrange slices of fontina cheese over the shells before pouring the sauce on top. As the shells bake, the fontina will melt beautifully.

10 ounces (about 33 individual) shells

1 pound ricotta cheese

1 1/2 cups coarsely grated Romano cheese

1 1/2 cups shredded mozzarella cheese

1 package (10 ounces) frozen spinach, thawed and chopped

2 eggs

1 teaspoon nutmeg

1 teaspoon coarsely ground black pepper

8 cups Famous Tomato Sauce (see p. 69)

SHELLS IN GOLD

Awash in a sea of gold, this dish looks truly spectacular. What's more, it tastes even better than it looks.

1. Cook the shells according to the package directions. Drain well and set aside in a large mixing bowl.

2. Place the saffron in the cup of chicken broth, stir, and set aside.

3. Cut the prosciutto into small cubes. Set aside.

4. Process the fontina in a food processor fitted with the steel blade until the cheese is chopped fine. Set aside.

5. Melt the butter in a saucepan over medium high heat. Add the flour to make a paste, or roux. Cook for 3 minutes. Whisking continuously, add the chicken broth and dissolved saffron, along with the salt.

6. Still whisking, add the milk. Reduce the heat. Add the grated nutmeg and cook for 5 minutes.

7. Add the finely chopped fontina and blend well. Remove the sauce from the heat.

8. Place 1/2 cup of the sauce in a small bowl or a cup. Mix in the beaten egg, whisking continuously.

9. Return the sauce and egg mixture to the saucepan. Whisk the sauce throughout.

10. Pour the sauce over the shells in the bowl. Add the Parmesan and the prosciutto and mix well. Transfer to a casserole dish. Bake at 400 degrees for 20 minutes.

1 pound medium shells

1/4 gram (1/2 teaspoon) saffron

1 cup chicken broth (homemade or canned)

1/2 pound prosciutto

1/2 pound Italian fontina cheese, sliced thick

3/4 cup (1 1/2 sticks) butter

1/2 cup flour

1/2 teaspoon salt

2 cups milk

1/2 whole nutmeg, grated

1 egg, beaten

1 1/2 cups grated Parmesan cheese

MACARONI AND CHEESE

Serves 4–6

It may have been the northern Italians who first baked a macaroni with cheese and cream, but almost as soon as Americans found out about this dish, we began to make it our own. Nineteenth-century versions of it often involved a tomato-and-meat sauce. How times have changed! Here's the macaroni and cheese that my family, and Cremaldi's customers, have been enjoying for years.

1. Cook the elbow macaroni according to package directions. Drain and transfer to a baking dish. Reserve.

2. Heat the milk, cream, and cheese together in a saucepan over low heat, stirring frequently.

3. When the cheese is thoroughly melted, pour the mixture over the macaroni. Blend. Top with bread crumbs and sprinkle with paprika. Bake in a 350-degree oven for 30 minutes.

1 pound elbow macaroni

2 cups milk

1 cup light cream or half-and-half

1 pound American cheese (preferably orange-colored), sliced in small pieces

1/2 cup plain bread crumbs

Paprika

RISOTTO WITH PORCINI AND ONIONS

Serves 4–6

Risotto is not so much a particular short-grain rice as the Italian technique for cooking it. Properly prepared risotto should absorb its cooking liquid slowly so that it can blend with other tastes and so that its texture becomes thick and chewy. There are probably as many ingredients you can combine with risotto as flavors for homemade macaroni, which is to say an unlimited number. This recipe offers one of my favorite combinations.

1. Place the rice in a 4-quart saucepan. Pour in enough chicken broth to a depth of 1 inch above it. Bring the broth and the rice to a rolling boil. Lower the heat, cover the pot, and cook for 15 minutes, making sure to remove the pot from the heat before all the broth is absorbed. Meanwhile, prepare the porcini.

2. Soak the porcini for 10 minutes in a cup of hot tap water to reconstitute. Then mix the soaking water into the cooked risotto and sliver the porcini.

3. Melt the butter in a skillet over medium heat. Add

1 package (500 grams) short-grain Italian rice

46 ounces (1 large can) chicken broth

1 cup (1 ounce) dried porcini mushrooms

1/2 cup (1 stick) butter

1 small onion, peeled and sliced

1 1/2 cups coarsely grated Parmesan cheese

the sliced onion and the slivered porcini and sauté for 10 minutes.

4. Transfer the mixture to a bowl and stir in the fried onion and porcini.

5. Bake in a 400-degree oven for 15 minutes. Remove from the oven, sprinkle the grated Parmesan over the top, cut the risotto like a lasagna, and serve.

VARIATIONS: Cook the rice in water instead of chicken broth. Then add 3 cups of your favorite red sauce to the risotto, onion, and porcini, mix in Romano instead of Parmesan, and don't bake the dish at all—just enjoy it right away. Another delicious variation is to mix in 1 cup slivered prosciutto.

GOOD OLD-FASHIONED SPAGHETTI AND MEATBALLS

Serves 4–6

Ever since the 1890s, when a factory on Staten Island in New York City began manufacturing dried spaghetti in quantity, spaghetti and meatballs has been a favorite American food. And this recipe, which comes from my father, is my favorite version of the dish. Like most other Italians, he always uses dry, packaged spaghetti to make it.

1. In a large bowl, combine the ground beef, eggs, parsley, pepper, cheese, bread crumbs, and minced garlic. Using your hands, mix thoroughly. When the ingredients are incorporated, roll out 6 meatballs, each about 1½ inches in diameter.

2. Heat the oil in a large skillet over medium high heat and then place the meatballs in the skillet. Allow each meatball to cook well on one side before turning. Then continue turning them until all sides are browned. Place the meatballs in the tomato sauce and heat in a separate skillet over a low flame for 10 to 15 minutes, or until the meatballs finish cooking. Meanwhile, cook the spaghetti.

3. Follow the package directions to cook the spaghetti. Drain well and transfer to a large platter.

4. Pour the tomato sauce over the spaghetti and mix together, using two forks. Top with the meatballs and a good grated Romano or Parmesan.

1 pound lean ground beef

2 eggs

1/2 cup coarsely chopped Italian parsley

1 heaping teaspoon coarsely ground black pepper

1 cup coarsely grated Romano cheese (plus more to sprinkle on top)

1/2 cup plain bread crumbs

1 large garlic clove, peeled and minced

1 cup oil

1 quart Famous Tomato Sauce (see p. 69)

1 pound spaghetti

POLENTA

During my childhood, polenta was the ultimate family meal. My grandmother would pour the cornmeal thick and hot onto a wooden board to cool. This board would be placed on the table, the polenta covered with sausage sauce, and then the whole family would sit down to slice pieces of it, all of us eating, as it were, from the same plate. You can eat the polenta plain, if you'd like, but it's really much better with the sausage sauce. Just be forewarned that the sauce takes longer to cook than the polenta does.

1. In a large pan over high heat, bring the water to a rolling boil. Add the salt.

2. Stirring constantly, preferably with a long-handled wooden spoon, gradually pour in the cornmeal. The mixture should be thick and smooth.

3. Reduce the heat to a simmer, cover the pan, and cook the polenta for about 35 minutes, stirring frequently.

4. Pour the polenta onto a wooden board and let cool.

5. To serve, simply slice and eat. Or cut the polenta into wedges, place the wedges in a baking pan, and cover them with a meat sauce, topped with coarsely grated Parmesan cheese. Bake the polenta in a 400-degree oven for about 10 minutes until it is lightly browned.

POLENTA
5 *cups water*
Pinch of salt
1½ *cups cornmeal*

1. In a saucepan, fry the sausage in the oil until brown.

2. Add the rest of the ingredients to the fried sausage. Stir well and simmer over medium heat for 1 hour 15 minutes.

3. Remove the pan from the heat. Cut the sausage into bite-sized pieces. Pour the sausage sauce over the polenta and serve.

SAUSAGE SAUCE
1 *pound Italian sweet fennel sausage (see p. 144)*
¼ *cup oil*
3 *cloves garlic, peeled and minced*
2 *pounds, 3 ounces (1 large can) whole peeled tomatoes, with juice*
6 *ounces (1 small can) tomato paste*
1 *teaspoon salt*
1 *teaspoon dried basil*
2 *teaspoons sugar*
2 *cups water*

TORTELLINI IN VODKA CREAM

Serves 4–6

This dish, which will help you celebrate the most special occasions, is practical as well as elegant. If there's enough sauce left, there's no reason tortellini in vodka cream can't be refrigerated and reheated in a skillet the next day.

1. Cook the tortellini. Drain well and transfer to a large serving bowl.

2. Melt the butter in a saucepan over medium high heat. Sprinkle in the crushed red pepper flakes. When the butter is bubbling rapidly, pour in the vodka. Simmer for 3 minutes.

3. Add the whole tomatoes and both grated cheeses. Simmer for 3 more minutes. Pour in the cream and simmer for 1 additional minute.

4. Remove the sauce from the heat. Pour the sauce over the tortellini and serve.

1 pound cheese tortellini

1/2 cup (1 stick) butter

1 teaspoon red pepper flakes

1/2 cup vodka

1 cup canned whole tomatoes, drained

3/4 cup coarsely grated Parmesan cheese

1/2 cup coarsely grated Romano cheese

1 cup heavy cream

SHELLS WITH BLUEBERRIES

Serves 4–6

You might think that this unusual fruit and cheese combination in a buttery tomato sauce was dreamed up by some nouvelle cuisine *chef, but actually this is a traditional Italian dish. Whatever its origins, whoever makes these wonderful shells with blueberries now will almost certainly receive a good deal of credit.*

1. Cook the shells according to the package directions. Drain and transfer to a mixing bowl.

2. Melt the butter in a saucepan over medium high heat. When the butter is sizzling, whisk in the tomato paste. Let simmer for 5 minutes, whisking often.

3. Whisk in the wine and lower the heat. Whisk in the sugar. Continue to simmer over low heat for 5 more minutes, whisking often.

4. Pour the hot sauce over the shells. Add the blueberries and mix through. Transfer the pasta mixture to a serving bowl. Sprinkle with the grated Gruyère and serve immediately.

1 pound medium shells

16 tablespoons (2 sticks) butter

12 ounces (2 cans) tomato paste

1 cup Burgundy or other dry red wine

1/2 teaspoon sugar

2 cups blueberries, fresh or frozen

1 cup grated Gruyère cheese

FUSILLI WITH CAULIFLOWER

Serves 4–6

Fusilli, which literally means "little springs," is also known as spindles, spirals, or just curly spaghetti. If you can find it, buy a spinach fusilli. Not only will the color and flavor mix beautifully with the cauliflower, but you will be making this one-dish meal even more nutritious.

1. If your cauliflower is fresh, quarter it and then break it up into small pieces. Place the pieces in a pot and cover them with water. Let the water boil for 15 minutes until the cauliflower is tender but not mushy. Drain and set aside. (If frozen, continue to thaw and then reserve the cauliflower.)

2. Heat the oil in a saucepan over medium high heat. Add the onions and cook until soft. If you're using them, cut up the anchovies now and mash them into the oil until they're melted in.

3. Add the tomatoes, pine nuts, currants, salt, and pepper. Simmer, uncovered, for 20 minutes.

4. Bring 5 quarts of water to a boil and drop in the fusilli. Cook until al dente, about 2 minutes, or according to package directions. Drain. Top with the sauce and serve.

1 small cauliflower **or** *1 package (8 ounces) frozen cauliflower, thawed*

4 tablespoons olive oil

1 large yellow onion, peeled and sliced

3 anchovy fillets (optional)

2 pounds canned whole tomatoes, with juice

1 tablespoon pine nuts

1 tablespoon dried currants

1 teaspoon salt

1 teaspoon coarsely ground black pepper

1 pound fusilli

ST. JOSEPH'S ANGEL HAIR

Serves 4–6

This light and delicate tangle of pasta is a traditional dish. It's required fare in Boston's Italian North End at least once a year, on St. Joseph's feast day, March 19, when—perhaps because of its sweetness—it is a particular favorite with the children. Of course, you can enjoy this angel hair any time, especially since it takes only a few minutes to prepare.

1. Bring 5 quarts of water to a boil in a large pot and cook the angel hair for 2 minutes. Rinse with cold water and drain.

2. In a bowl, using your hand or a fork, combine the

1/2 pound dried angel hair pasta

2 cups plain bread crumbs

1 heaping tablespoon ground cinnamon

bread crumbs, cinnamon, garlic, parsley, salt, and 1/4 cup of the oil.

3. In another bowl, toss the angel hair with the remaining 1/4 cup oil to loosen and moisten the pasta.

4. Blend the bread crumb mixture with the angel hair. Toss thoroughly, to coat all the pasta, yet gently, trying not to break the individual strands. Serve at once or refrigerate.

3 large garlic cloves, peeled and minced fine

1 1/2 cups coarsely chopped Italian parsley

1 teaspoon salt

1/2 cup oil

CHEESE TORTELLINI SALAD IN PESTO

Serves 4–6

This pasta salad, probably the most popular on our regular lunch menu, is perfect for a spring or summer party buffet. Its pretty colors are inviting, its taste irresistible. Try to use fresh tortellini, if you can.

1. Bring 5 quarts of water to a boil in a large pot, stir in the tortellini, and cook until al dente (6 minutes for fresh tortellini). Rinse the pasta with cold water, drain well, and place in a large bowl.

2. Pour the oil over the tortellini and mix through. Add the halved cherry tomatoes, quartered olives, artichoke hearts, Pesto Sauce, and cheese. Season with the pepper. Toss well and serve at room temperature.

1 pound cheese tortellini, fresh or dried

1/4 cup oil

1 pint cherry tomatoes, cut in half

6 ounces (1 can) pitted black olives, quartered

8 1/2 ounces (1 can or jar) artichoke hearts in brine, drained and quartered

1 cup Pesto Sauce (see p. 75)

1/2 cup coarsely grated Parmesan cheese

1 teaspoon coarsely ground black pepper

MEDITERRANEAN SALAD

Serves 4–6

The red, white, and green of the Italian flag are saluted in this attractive and popular summer salad. Mediterranean Salad is best when served immediately, so if you must make it in advance, don't actually assemble it until the last minute. It's perfect for lunch or a light supper, needing only a chilled bottle of wine and a loaf of crusty bread as accompaniment.

1. Bring 5 quarts of water to a boil in a large pot and cook the rotini for about 8 minutes. Rinse with cold water and drain. In a large serving bowl, moisten the rotini with 1/4 cup of the oil.

2. Cut the salami in small pieces. Slice the olives in thirds. Slice the scallions in 1/4-inch pieces. Quarter the mushrooms. Toss these ingredients with the rotini. Sprinkle in the almonds.

3. Pour the mushroom marinade, the remaining 1/4 cup oil, and vinegar over the salad. Season with the tarragon, black pepper, garlic powder, and salt. Toss well and serve.

1 pound rotini
1/2 cup oil
1/4 pound salami, in a chunk or sliced
6 ounces (1 can) pitted black olives
3/4 cup (about 6) scallions
8 ounces (1 jar) marinated mushrooms, including marinade
1 cup slivered almonds
3 tablespoons red wine vinegar
5 tablespoons dried tarragon
1 tablespoon coarsely ground black pepper
1/2 teaspoon garlic powder
1 teaspoon salt

WHAT WOULD WE DO WITHOUT BREAD, THE STAFF of life? When I was growing up, there was always toasted bread with butter for breakfast and melted cheese over bread for lunch and bread dipped in egg on one side and fried in oil whenever my brother and I got hungry. Usually we had sliced Wonder bread like all the other kids, but sometimes we feasted on my grandmother's homemade Italian loaves. To this day, it's the only truly wonderful bread I've ever eaten.

When my mother was a child, my grandmother, Louisa Colaiuta, baked bread at least twice a week in her own wood-burning brick oven in the backyard. She would stoke the fire, swish out the hot oven with a bucket of water, and test its heat by throwing a bit of flour in and watching to see it change color. Only then would my grandmother set the unbaked loaves inside and close the oven's wooden door for about an hour. If the bread was baking too quickly, she used a stick to prop the door slightly open; there were no gauges to go by. Whatever she did must have been just right: my mother says that her mother's bread was always perfect.

Louisa remained a devoted breadmaker her whole life, even after my grandfather built our family's house where the brick oven had stood and all the baking had to be done indoors. She would still proof her yeast in warm water the night before and begin her kneading by five the next morning. Working as much as twenty-five pounds of flour in her huge wooden bowl, she would use her two fists to knead and knead until the dough was very soft, but not sticky, and as smooth as silk. After letting it rise, there was more kneading and a rise again. Then my grandmother would cut her loaves.

It wasn't just the soft insides or the crunchy outsides that made Louisa's bread so special. It wasn't even the way we usually ate the bread—straight from the oven, steamy hot, and covered with olive oil. What really fascinated me about my grandmother's bread was the dough itself, or, more precisely, how she transformed it. Sometimes she would fry salt pork for my grandfather and mix in the crispy chunks as she was kneading. Other times she would shape the dough like fat little men, delighting my brother and me. Once in a while she would put the dough into a round pan, cover it with sliced fresh garden tomatoes, and bake her cakepan pizza. And on those rare occasions when her bread would go stale, she would revive it by pouring boiled scallions and potatoes over the hard leftover chunks and sprinkling this makeshift soup with plenty of grated Romano.

My grandmother could work wonders with bread and so can you. In this chapter, you'll see how easy it is to take your dough and shape it to any size pan, deep or shallow, round or square, thick or thin. Of course, most supermarkets these days sell frozen dough and many bakeries have dough already prepared, but following our all-purpose dough recipe is easier, cheaper, and much more rewarding. Not only does this recipe make great rolls and pies but also, with a little help from toppings and fillings, an unlimited number of large and small pizzas as well as those irresistible turnovers called calzone. There is nothing more fulfilling for a cook than putting so few ingredients into a bowl and watching them grow into something that smells divine and looks fantastic. So go forth with this basic recipe and make it multiply! ◆

ALL-PURPOSE DOUGH

Makes 1 pound dough

This is the only recipe you'll ever need to make a basic bread, pizza, or calzone.

BY HAND

1. In a large stainless steel or porcelain bowl (15–18 inches in diameter), place the water, yeast, and salt.

2. When the yeast is dissolved, add 2 cups of the flour. Using four fingers of one hand, start in the middle of the bowl and make widening concentric circles to incorporate the flour gradually into the yeast mixture. It will be sticky.

3. Add the other 1/2 cup flour and begin kneading the mixture in the bowl until the dough is smooth and elastic, about 5 minutes.

4. The sides of the bowl should be fairly clean of dough by this time. Form dough into a ball, then place

1 cup warm tap water (110 degrees)

1 package active dry yeast

1/4 teaspoon salt

2 1/2 cups all-purpose flour

the dough back in the same bowl and cover bowl with plastic wrap. Set the bowl in a warm, draft-free place for 1 hour or until the dough has doubled in bulk. (If the dough has not begun to rise after an hour, throw it out and start again.)

5. Punch down the doubled dough and roll it into any shape you desire.

BY FOOD PROCESSOR

1. Place the water, yeast, and salt in a food processor fitted with the steel blade. Turn the processor on and off a couple of times to dissolve the yeast.

2. Add all the flour and process until the dough forms a ball. (If the dough seems too sticky, add 2 tablespoons more flour and run the machine until the dough forms a ball again.)

3. Place the ball of dough in a bowl and cover with plastic wrap. Set the bowl in a warm, draft-free place for 1 hour and let it rise. (Here, too, if the dough has not begun to rise after an hour, throw it out and start again.)

4. When the dough has doubled in bulk, punch it down and roll it into the desired shape.

NOTE: This dough can be refrigerated for up to five days; it also freezes nicely.

To refrigerate: Punch down the dough after it rises and instead of rolling it, refrigerate immediately. When you're ready to roll it, let the dough sit for 40 minutes at room temperature first.

To freeze: Punch down the dough after it rises, place it in a freezer bag, and freeze. When you're ready to use the dough, take it out of the freezer and place it in the refrigerator overnight or longer, until thawed. Then set the dough in a warm, draft-free place until the dough is room temperature. (It is also possible to thaw the dough quickly by transferring it directly from the freezer to a very warm, draft-free place.)

FRANK BELLOTTI'S LONG ITALIAN BREAD

Makes 2 loaves bread

Cooking is definitely a great love in the life of Frank Bellotti, the former attorney general of Massachusetts. Every Sunday he wakes up at 3 A.M. to start cooking for his twelve children and at least half a dozen other people. Mr. Bellotti is busy in his kitchen more frequently than just Sunday mornings. Among other things, he bakes ten loaves of his long Italian bread in double French loaf pans each week. With such dedication, maybe Mr. Bellotti should be writing this book instead of me.

1. Place the flour and salt in a large stainless steel bowl. Mix thoroughly.

2. Pour the yeast, sugar, and warm water into a large, clear drinking glass or small bowl. When the yeast dissolves and bubbles (in about 3–5 minutes), it is proofed.

3. Add the proofed yeast mixture to the flour and salt in the stainless steel bowl. Add the cold water. With a wooden spoon, mix thoroughly until a fairly firm dough forms, adding more flour if necessary.

4. Turn the dough out on a lightly floured surface and knead 3–5 minutes, "slamming" the dough on the table, Mr. Bellotti says, as you knead.

5. Grease a bowl with oil. Place the dough inside the bowl and turn it so that the outside of the dough is completely coated with the oil. Cover the bowl with plastic wrap and set it in an unlit gas oven (or another warm, draft-free place) for 1 hour, or until the dough has doubled in bulk.

6. Punch down the dough and divide it in half. Grease a double French loaf pan with oil, and shape the dough to fit. Sprinkle flour on top of the loaves. Cover the loaves with plastic wrap and a towel and let rise a second time in a warm, draft-free place for about 40 minutes or until the loaves have doubled in bulk again.

7. Preheat the oven for 10 minutes to 500 degrees. Spray the inside bottom of the oven ten or fifteen times with water, using a plant mister. Sprinkle more flour on top of the loaves. (This will help give the bread a crunchy crust.) Then set the loaves on the middle rack in the oven and bake for 7 minutes. (Mr. Bellotti is precise.)

4 cups all-purpose flour (plus more for sprinkling)

1 tablespoon salt

1 package dry yeast

1/4 teaspoon sugar

1/2 cup very warm water (110 degrees)

1 1/2 cups cold water

vegetable oil

8. Spray the bottom of the oven with water a few more times. Bake the loaves for 10 additional minutes.

9. Reduce the temperature of the oven to 400 degrees. Spray the bottom of the oven one more time. Bake the breads for 21 minutes more.

FOCACCIA

Serves 4–6

Italians have been eating focaccia ever since Roman times. No wonder. The vision of this spongy soft bread, not to mention the heavenly fragrance of its herbs, makes you want to devour the whole thing. I like to cut focaccia in squares and serve it in a pretty basket alongside a good hearty soup or stew.

1. Warm the milk to lukewarm and pour it into a very large bowl. Sprinkle in the sugar, dried herbs, black pepper, and yeast. Stir gently. Let the mixture stand for about 5 minutes until the yeast bubbles and foams.

2. Using a wooden spoon, mix in the salt and flour. Then add ½ cup of the olive oil and the chopped onion to the dough. Cover the bowl with a towel and set it in a warm, draft-free spot to rise for about an hour, until it doubles in bulk or until your finger can make a permanent hole in the dough.

3. When the dough has risen, incorporate the remaining ¼ cup oil. Punch down the dough and turn it out onto a cookie sheet, fitting the dough across the sheet. Cover again with a towel and let the dough rise in a warm, draft-free spot for 30 minutes more.

4. Bake the focaccia on the cookie sheet in a 400-degree oven for 30 minutes. Let it cool for 15 minutes and cut into 4-inch squares to serve.

2 cups milk

1 teaspoon sugar

2 teaspoons dried oregano

2 teaspoons dried basil

2 teaspoons dried thyme or rosemary

2 teaspoons dried parsley

1 teaspoon coarsely ground black pepper

¼ ounce (1 package) active dry yeast

2 teaspoons salt

3 cups flour

¾ cup extra virgin olive oil

¾ medium yellow onion, peeled and chopped

PANINI

We serve these rolls or "little breads" with soup or salad for lunch every day at the store. They also make great mini-sandwiches. I'd like to have them later in the day as well, but no matter how many panini we make, by the end of lunch they've all disappeared.

1. Shape the dough into an oval. Cut the oval into six pieces.

2. Shape each piece of dough by rolling it between the palms of your hands into an oblong chunk measuring approximately 3 × 2 inches.

3. Mix the egg with a tablespoon of water to create a wash. Brush the top of each panini with the wash and then sprinkle the tops with poppy or sesame seeds.

1 pound All-purpose Dough (see p. 00)

1 egg, beaten
  Poppy seeds or sesame seeds
  Oil for cookie sheet

Brush the panini with an egg-water mixture and sprinkle with sesame or poppy seeds.

4. Place the panini on an oiled cookie sheet and bake in a 400-degree oven for 20 minutes, or until light brown.

VARIATIONS: Before baking the panini, place a chunk of your favorite cheese up through the bottom of each piece of dough. You can also vary the look and taste of the panini by sprinkling coarsely ground black pepper, dried herbs, or red pepper flakes on the tops.

FRIED DOUGH

Makes about 6 pieces fried dough

Here's an old Italian favorite, enjoyed at any and every time of day. Many people like their fried dough for dessert, sweetened in sugar or spread with jam; my father covers his fried dough with peanut butter when he wants to treat himself to a really nourishing breakfast. Personally, I like eating my fried dough sprinkled with salt. For me, the simplest way to serve a food is often the best. Experiment to find your own favorite way to enjoy this treat.

1. Pour both oils into an 8-inch skillet, until the skillet is half full. Heat the oils over medium high heat. Meanwhile, prepare your pieces of dough.

2. Break off pieces of dough the size of the palm of your hand. Flatten each piece with your hands until it is 1/2 to 1 inch thick. With a fork, prick the top of each piece of dough all over.

3. When the oil is very hot, but not smoking, begin to fry the dough. Cook as many pieces as you can fit in the skillet at the same time. When the pieces become light brown on one side, turn them. When the other side is also light brown, transfer the fried dough to a paper towel to drain. Sprinkle or spread with whatever you'd like and serve immediately.

1¹/2 cups olive oil
1¹/2 cups vegetable oil
1 pound All-purpose Dough (see pp. 108–109)

TARALLI

Like fried dough, there are many ways to enjoy taralli. My husband, Cosmo, can remember his father putting taralli in a soup bowl and then pouring in coffee to soften the hard, flavored bread. Cosmo's mother would dunk the taralli in her coffee cup like a doughnut. This particular recipe for the traditional Italian treat comes courtesy of former Massachusetts Attorney General Frank Bellotti.

1. Take 1 cup of the flour and mix it with the dry yeast. Set aside.

2. Beat the eggs with the olive oil in a medium-sized bowl. Set aside.

3. Mix the remaining 3 cups of flour with the anise seed and pepper in a large bowl. Set aside.

4. Take the flour and yeast mixture and combine it with the egg mixture. With a fork, mix together to form a well-incorporated, thick paste.

5. Add to this paste the flour, anise, and pepper mixture. With a wooden spoon or your hand, mix until the dough comes together in the bowl.

6. Turn out the dough onto a floured work surface and knead about 3 minutes, until the flour is well incorporated and the dough looks fairly smooth. Shape the dough into a ball and cover this ball with a bowl to prevent drying out.

7. Fill an 8-quart pot with water and bring to a boil.

8. Take a chunk of dough, a little smaller than a walnut, and make a ball. Roll the ball on your work surface into a cigar shape about 6 inches long. Bring the ends of the cigar together in the shape of a teardrop. Pinch the ends firmly together to seal. Shape about a dozen taralli at a time this way.

9. When the water is boiling, drop the taralli into the pot. When the taralli surface, remove each one with a slotted spoon and drain it on a paper towel. Transfer the drained taralli to a cookie sheet.

10. Repeat steps 8 and 9 until you have used all the dough and filled a cookie sheet.

4 cups all-purpose flour

1/4 ounce (1 package) active dry yeast

6 eggs

1/2 cup olive oil

1 teaspoon whole anise seeds

1 teaspoon coarsely ground black pepper

11. Bake the taralli in a 400-degree oven for 40 minutes or until they are golden brown. Cool completely before serving. (You can also store the taralli in a plastic bag. They keep for a long time.)

PIZZA

Ever since the first pizzeria opened in New York City in 1905, touting a secret family recipe, Americans have been individualizing their pizzas. Some people like a classic pizza consisting of just a thin, crisp crust, tomato sauce, cheese, and a hint of oregano, while others feel the thicker and chewier the crust the better, and load it with vegetables, slices of meat, anchovies, goat cheese, and any other ingredients that are available. There's at least one exception to this ongoing pizza personalization, though. Everyone agrees that the pizza Rosie makes every day at our store is about the best they've ever tasted. They say that the thick, chewy crust with the crispy, crunchy edges is always perfect.

Here is the recipe for Rosie's pizza. If you want your crust thicker still, simply use more dough, say a pound and a half; if you want it thinner, use less. And as for individualizing, only the crust ingredients remain the same. You choose the shape of your pizza and you choose the toppings (or, in the case of covered pizza, the fillings). This way you can make every pizza baked in your oven uniquely your own.

Here are the directions for forming the different pizza shapes. The recipes for the toppings and fillings follow separately.

LARGE COOKIE-SHEET PIZZA

1 pound All-purpose Dough (see pp. 108–109)
Oil for pan
Topping ingredients

1. Roll out the dough into a rectangle about an inch longer and an inch wider than a cookie sheet measuring 17¼ × 11½ × 1 inches. Oil the sheet. Fit the dough across the sheet. Leave about an inch of dough overlapping the edges of the sheet. With your fingers, lift and roll the overlapping dough up over the edges of the sheet to form a thick ridge along the edges.

2. Assemble the topping on the pizza.

3. Bake the pizza in a 400-degree oven for 30 minutes or until golden brown.

Makes 1 large pizza; serves 4–6

ROUND PIZZA

1. Roll out the dough into a circle about an inch larger than a round pizza pan measuring 12 to 15 inches in diameter. Oil the pan. Fit the dough into the pan. Leave about an inch of dough overlapping the edge of the pan. With your fingers, lift and roll the overlapping dough up over the edge of the pan to form a thick ridge around it.

2. Assemble the topping on the pizza.

3. Bake the pizza in a 400-degree oven for 30 minutes or until golden brown.

Makes 1 large pizza; serves 4–6

INDIVIDUAL PIZZAS

1. Shape the dough into an oval. Slice the dough into three pieces. Flatten each piece of dough until it becomes a circle about 1½ inch thick and 4 inches in diameter, or ½ inch thick and 6 inches in diameter. Place these three pizzas on an oiled cookie sheet.

2. Assemble the toppings on the individual pizzas.

3. Bake the pizzas in a 400-degree oven for 30 minutes or until golden brown.

Makes 3 individual pizzas; serves 3–6

COVERED PIZZA

2 pounds All-purpose Dough (see pp. 108–109)
Olive oil to brush the top crust

1. Divide the dough in half. Roll out each portion of dough into a rectangle about an inch longer and an inch wider than a cookie sheet measuring 17¼ × 11½ × 1 inches. Oil the sheet. Fit one rectangle across the sheet, leaving about an inch of dough overlapping the edges.

2. Spread the filling evenly across the dough on the cookie sheet.

3. Place the other rectangle of dough over the filling. Then lift and roll the overlapping dough up over the edges of the cookie sheet to form a thick ridge.

4. Brush the top of the pizza with olive oil. Make several slits on top of the pizza to help steam to escape. Then bake in a 400-degree oven for 30 minutes or until the top is golden brown.

Makes 1 large covered pizza; serves 4–6

BASIC TOMATO PIZZA SAUCE

Makes 2 cups sauce

Combine all of the ingredients in a food processor fitted with the steel blade. Process until smooth.

1 *large fresh tomato*

1 *cup canned whole tomatoes, without juice*

1 *teaspoon dried oregano*

1 *teaspoon dried basil*

1/2 *teaspoon salt*

1/2 *teaspoon coarsely ground black pepper*

1/4 *cup olive oil*

PESTO PIZZA

Makes 1 large rectangular pizza

1. Shape the dough to fit an oiled cookie sheet. Leave about an inch of dough overlapping the edges of the sheet. Roll the overlapping dough up over the edges to form a thick ridge.

2. Place the slices of American cheese on top of the dough. Spread the pesto sauce over the cheese. Cover the pesto with the slices of mozzarella.

3. Bake the pizza at 400 degrees for 30 minutes, or until golden brown.

1 *pound All-purpose Dough (see pp. 108–109)*

Oil for cookie sheet

12 *slices American cheese*

2 *cups Pesto Sauce (see p. 75)*

12 *slices mozzarella cheese*

FRESH BASIL AND TOMATO PIZZA

Makes 3 individual pizzas

1. Shape the dough into three small circles about 1 inch thick and 4 inches in diameter. Place the circles on an oiled cookie sheet.

2. Pour 1 teaspoon of oil over each pizza. Sprinkle each pizza with salt. Then place one slice of mozzarella on each pizza and spread a heaping tablespoon of pesto over each slice. Arrange a fresh tomato slice on each pizza and top with a sprinkling of black pepper.

3. Bake the pizzas at 400 degrees for 30 minutes, or until golden brown.

1/4 cup vegetable oil, plus oil for cookie sheet

3 large yellow onions, peeled and sliced

3 tablespoons sugar

2 pounds All-purpose Dough (see pp. 108–109)

12 slices mozzarella cheese

12 slices provolone cheese

Olive oil to brush the top crust

SWEET ONION PIZZA

Makes 1 large covered pizza

1. Heat the oil in a skillet over medium high heat. Add the onions and sauté for 5 minutes until the onions begin to turn golden.

2. Add the sugar, reduce the heat, and sauté the onions slowly for 25 minutes, turning often.

3. Meanwhile, roll out each pound of dough into a rectangle an inch larger than your cookie sheet. Lay one rectangle on the oiled sheet.

4. Arrange the mozzarella slices on top of the dough on the cookie sheet. Place the provolone on top of the mozzarella.

5. When the onions are cooked, pour them over the cheeses. Cover the filling with the other rectangle of dough and seal by lifting the overlapping dough up over the edges of the cookie sheet to form a thick ridge.

6. Brush the top of the pizza with olive oil and make slits for steam to escape. Bake at 400 degrees for 30 minutes or until golden brown.

1 pound All-purpose Dough (see pp. 108–109)

3 teaspoons oil (plus oil for cookie sheet)

Salt

3 slices mozzarella cheese

3 heaping tablespoons Pesto Sauce (see p. 75)

3 slices fresh tomato, 1/2 inch thick

Coarsely ground black pepper

HAM AND SWISS WITH HONEY MUSTARD PIZZA

Makes 3 individual pizzas

1. Shape the dough into three small circles about 1 inch thick and 4 inches in diameter. Place the circles on an oiled cookie sheet.

2. Sprinkle each circle of dough with a little salt. Place one slice of ham on each circle. Spread each ham slice with a teaspoon of honey mustard and a sprinkling of oregano and basil, then fold the slice of ham in half. Cover with a tomato slice and top with grated Swiss cheese.

3. Bake the pizzas at 400 degrees for 30 minutes or until golden brown.

4. Remove the cooked pizzas from the oven and decorate the top of each one with an olive and vinegared pepper, sliced into thin strips. (The peppers should not be omitted. The combination of the sweetness of the honey mustard and the saltiness of the peppers is especially good.)

1 pound All-purpose Dough (see pp. 108–109)
Oil for cookie sheet
Salt
3 slices boiled ham
3 teaspoons honey mustard
Dried oregano
Dried basil
1 tomato, cut in slices each 1/3 inch thick
1/2 cup coarsely grated Swiss cheese
3 oil-cured olives, pitted
1 red vinegared pepper (available in jars at many supermarkets and Italian specialty shops)

HAM AND CHEESE PIZZA

Makes 1 large covered pizza

1. Roll out each pound of dough into a rectangle an inch larger than your cookie sheet. Lay one rectangle on the oiled sheet.

2. Cover the dough with the Danish ham, then add a layer of provolone. Next sprinkle on the chopped onions and diced salami, and top with a layer of Swiss cheese and finally a layer of fontina.

3. In a bowl, beat the eggs. Combine with the Romano and parsley. Pour this mixture over the filling already on the dough and spread evenly.

4. Cover the entire filling with the other rectangle of dough and seal by lifting the overlapping dough up over the edges of the cookie sheet to form a thick ridge.

5. Brush the top crust with olive oil and make slits for steam to escape. Bake at 400 degrees for 30 minutes or until golden brown.

2 pounds All-purpose Dough (see pp. 108–109)

Oil for cookie sheet

8 slices Danish ham

8 slices provolone cheese

1 large onion, peeled and finely chopped

15 slices salami, diced

8 slices Swiss cheese

8 slices Italian fontina cheese

6 eggs

1 cup coarsely grated Romano cheese

1 cup coarsely chopped Italian parsley

Olive oil to brush the top crust

GRANDMA'S CAKEPAN PIZZA

Serves 4–6

This was the only way my grandmother ever made pizza, and before I moved to Cambridge, Massachusetts, the only way I ever knew pizza could be made. It's thick, puffy, chewy, and flavorful.

1. Grease an 8- or 10-inch round cakepan or an iron skillet with 1 tablespoon of the oil.

2. Press the dough so that it fits snugly into the bottom of the cakepan.

3. Cover the dough completely with all of the tomato slices. Sprinkle the basil, pepper, minced garlic, and salt over the tomatoes.

4. Drizzle the remaining 2 tablespoons of oil over the top of the tomatoes and bake the pizza in a 400-degree oven for 30 minutes, or until golden brown.

3 tablespoons oil

1 pound All-purpose Dough (see pp. 108–109)

1 or 2 fresh tomatoes, cut in 1/2-inch slices

2 tablespoons chopped fresh basil **or** 2 tablespoons chopped fresh Italian parsley

1/4 teaspoon coarsely ground black pepper

4 garlic cloves, minced

1/4 teaspoon salt

THREE-PEPPER PIZZA

Makes 1 large rectangular or round pizza

1. Oil a cookie sheet or pizza pan and shape the dough to fit. Leave an inch of dough overlapping the edges of the sheet or pan. Roll the overlapping dough up over the edges to form a thick ridge.

2. Spread the salsa over the dough. Drizzle the ¼ cup oil over the salsa.

3. Layer all of the Cheddar and all of the mozzarella cheese on top of the pizza.

4. Arrange the strips of yellow, green, and red peppers on top of the cheese.

5. Sprinkle the basil and the black pepper over the pizza. Bake at 400 degrees for 30 minutes, or until golden brown.

PIZZA

Oil for pan

1 pound All-purpose Dough (see pp. 108–109)

Salsa, homemade (see below) or commercial

¼ cup olive oil

12 slices Cheddar cheese

12 slices mozzarella cheese

3 bell peppers—1 yellow, 1 green, 1 red, sliced in thin strips

2 teaspoons dried basil

1 tablespoon coarsely ground black pepper

1. Combine the bell peppers and onions in a food processor fitted with the steel blade. Process on "pulse" until the vegetables are coarse, about 30 seconds.

2. Add the tomatoes, jalapeño pepper, cilantro, cumin, and salt and continue to process on "pulse" until all of the vegetables are the same consistency. A word of caution: handle the jalapeño pepper as little as possible and wash your hands thoroughly immediately after touching the pepper. It will leave a residue that stings the skin.

SALSA

1 red, 1 yellow, and 1 green bell pepper, stemmed, seeded and cut in half

1 red onion, peeled and quartered

1 yellow onion, peeled and quartered

2 large ripe red tomatoes

1 fresh or jarred jalapeño pepper, seeded

½ cup chopped fresh cilantro

1 tablespoon ground cumin

Salt to taste

TOMATO AND CHEESE PIZZA

Makes 1 large rectangular or round pizza

1. Oil a cookie sheet or pizza pan and shape the dough to fit. Leave an inch of dough overlapping the edges of the sheet or pan. Roll the overlapping dough up over the edges to form a thick ridge.

2. Arrange the slices of American cheese in three rows, covering the dough.

3. Using your hand, squash the tomatoes over the cheese. (You can also pour on a little of the reserved juice from the tomatoes.)

4. Sprinkle the oregano, black pepper, and garlic powder over the tomatoes. Top the pizza by sprinkling on the Romano. Bake at 400 degrees for 30 minutes or until golden brown.

Oil for pan

1 pound All-purpose Dough (see pp. 108–109)

12 slices American cheese

1 can (1 pound, 12 ounces) whole tomatoes, peeled, with some juice reserved

1 tablespoon dried oregano

1 tablespoon coarsely ground black pepper

1 tablespoon garlic powder

2 cups coarsely grated Romano cheese

BUFFALO MOZZARELLA PIZZA

Makes 1 large rectangular pizza

1. Oil a cookie sheet and shape the dough to fit. Leave an inch of dough overlapping the edges of the sheet. Roll the overlapping dough up over the edges to form a thick ridge.

2. Spread ½ cup of the pizza sauce over the dough. Arrange all 12 slices of American cheese over the sauce. Cover the cheese with the other half cup of sauce. Then lay down the slices of buffalo mozzarella. Top with the chopped parsley and sprinkle on the black pepper.

3. Bake the pizza at 400 degrees for 30 minutes, or until golden brown.

Oil for cookie sheet

1 pound All-purpose Dough (see pp. 108–109)

1 cup Basic Tomato Pizza Sauce (see p. 117)

12 slices American cheese

1½–2 pounds buffalo mozzarella cheese, sliced

1 cup coarsely chopped Italian parsley

1 tablespoon coarsely ground black pepper

PARMIGIANA PIZZA

Makes 1 large rectangular pizza

1. Oil a cookie sheet and shape the dough to fit. Leave an inch of dough overlapping the edges. Roll the overlapping dough up over the edges to form a thick ridge.

2. Spread ½ cup pizza sauce over the dough. Place the slices of mozzarella over the sauce. Cover the mozzarella with the other ½ cup of sauce. Then sprinkle on the grated Parmesan.

3. Bake the pizza at 400 degrees for 30 minutes or until golden brown.

Oil for cookie sheet

1 pound All-purpose Dough (see pp. 108–109)

1 cup Basic Tomato Pizza Sauce (see p. 117)

12 slices mozzarella cheese

2 cups coarsely grated Parmesan cheese

FOUR SEASONS ROUND PIZZA

Makes 1 large round pizza

1. Oil a pizza pan and shape the dough into a circle to fit. Leave about an inch of dough overlapping the edge of the pan. Roll the overlapping dough up all around the edge to form a thick ridge.

2. Spread ⅛ cup pizza sauce over the dough. Place all 12 slices of American cheese over the sauce. Cover the cheese with the remaining sauce. Then sprinkle on the grated mozzarella.

3. On top of the mozzarella, place all 24 tomato wedges, skin side down, to make a large X that crisscrosses the pizza. The pizza will now be divided into four sections.

4. Bake the pizza at 400 degrees for 25 minutes. Remove from oven.

5. Place the prosciutto in one section, the mushrooms in another section, the artichoke hearts in a third section, and the olives in the last section of the pizza.

6. Return the pizza to the oven and bake at 400 degrees for 5 minutes more.

Oil for pan

1 pound All-purpose Dough (see pp. 108–109)

¼ cup Basic Tomato Pizza Sauce (see p. 117)

12 slices American cheese

4 cups grated mozzarella cheese

4 fresh tomatoes, each cut into 6 wedges

6 thin slices prosciutto

1½ cups fresh mushrooms

1½ cups marinated artichoke hearts, drained and sliced in half

1½ cups black olives, sliced in thirds

SAUSAGE PIZZA

Makes 1 large rectangular pizza

1. Oil a cookie sheet and shape the dough to fit. Leave about an inch of dough overlapping the edges of the sheet. Roll the overlapping dough up over the edges to form a thick ridge.

2. Spread ½ cup pizza sauce over the dough. Place all 12 slices of American cheese over the sauce. Spread the other half cup of sauce over the cheese.

3. Add the pieces of sausage to the pizza. Top with a layer of mozzarella cheese.

4. Bake the pizza at 400 degrees for 30 minutes or until golden brown.

Oil for cookie sheet

1 pound All-purpose Dough (see pp. 108–109)

1 cup Basic Tomato Pizza Sauce (see p. 117)

12 slices American cheese

1 pound sweet Italian sausages (see p. 114), cooked and sliced in ¼-inch pieces

12 slices mozzarella cheese

GORGONZOLA PIZZA

Makes 3 individual pizzas

1. Shape the dough into three small circles about ½ inch thick and 6 inches in diameter. Place the circles on an oiled cookie sheet.

2. Spread ⅛ cup pizza sauce in a thin coating over the three circles of dough. Place 3 slices of American cheese over the sauce on each pizza. Cover the cheese with the remaining sauce. If you'd like, arrange 3 slices of prosciutto on each pizza.

3. Place the chunks of Gorgonzola over each pizza. Top the pizzas by sprinkling ½ cup of grated Cheddar over each.

4. Bake the pizzas at 400 degrees for 30 minutes, or until golden brown.

1 pound All-purpose Dough (see pp. 108–109)

Oil for cookie sheet

¼ cup Basic Tomato Pizza Sauce (see p. 117)

9 slices American cheese

9 thin slices prosciutto (optional)

¾ pound Gorgonzola cheese, cut in 1-inch chunks

1½ cups grated Cheddar cheese

ARTICHOKE AND VINEGARED PEPPERS PIZZA

Makes 3 individual pizzas

1. Shape the dough into three small circles about ½ inch thick and 6 inches in diameter. Place the circles on an oiled cookie sheet.

2. Spread ⅛ cup pizza sauce in a thin coating over the three circles of dough. Place 3 slices of American cheese over the sauce on each pizza. Cover the cheese with the remaining sauce.

3. Distribute the slices of artichoke hearts evenly on each pizza and cover with 3 slices of mozzarella on each.

4. Bake the pizzas at 400 degrees for 30 minutes or until golden brown. Remove from oven and decorate each pizza with the vinegared pepper, sliced into thin strips.

1 pound All-purpose Dough (see pp. 108–109)
Oil for cookie sheet
½ cup Basic Tomato Pizza Sauce (see p. 117)
9 slices American cheese
12 artichoke hearts in brine, drained and quartered
9 slices mozzarella cheese
1 red vinegared pepper (available in jars at many supermarkets and Italian specialty shops)

TORTA RUSTICA

Serves 4–6

The name of this dish, which suggests a kind of homey simplicity, may be ironic, since torta rustica is really the most elegant pizza of all.

1. Divide the pound of dough in half. Roll out each piece of dough into a circle about an inch larger than a 6-inch cakepan. Oil the pan. Fit one circle of dough into the pan, leaving about an inch of dough overlapping the pan's edge.

2. In a large bowl, combine the eggs with the ricotta. Add the parsley, black pepper, and ziti. Then add the salami and provolone. Mix very well.

3. Place the filling in the dough inside the cakepan.

4. Fit the other circle of dough over the filling. Then lift and roll the edges up to form a ridge around the pan.

5. Brush the top of the torta with olive oil and bake in a 400-degree oven for 30 minutes, or until golden brown.

1 pound All-purpose Dough (see pp. 108–109)
Oil for pan
3 eggs, beaten
½ pound ricotta cheese
2 tablespoons coarsely chopped Italian parsley
1 teaspoon coarsely ground black pepper
¼ pound ziti, cooked al dente
¼ pound salami, diced
¼ pound provolone cheese, diced
Olive oil to brush the top crust

VEGETABLE TORTA

Serves 4–8

Like a well-designed building, this torta with its buttery crust and beautiful blend of bright colors is as impressive outside as it is irresistible inside. Use a deep round cakepan measuring 8 inches in diameter and at least 3 inches deep, so that the layers will have height as well as wonderful flavor.

1. In a bowl, combine the ricotta, eggs, parsley, 1 teaspoon of the black pepper, and the Romano or Parmesan. Mix well and set aside.

2. In a 10-inch skillet, melt 4 tablespoons (½ stick) of the butter over medium high heat. Add the onions and sauté until they begin to turn brown. Add the mushrooms and zucchini and cook until the zucchini is fairly soft, about 6 minutes. Remove the mixture from the skillet with a slotted spoon, drain off the juice, and reserve the sautéed vegetables.

3. Melt the remaining butter in the same skillet over medium high heat. Add the spinach and season with the other ¼ teaspoon of black pepper and the garlic powder, salt, and red pepper. Put a lid on the skillet and sauté for 5 minutes, stirring occasionally, until the spinach leaves are wilted and cooked through. Remove spinach mixture from heat, drain well, and reserve.

4. Place the halved red and yellow peppers on a cookie sheet, skin side up. Roast the peppers in a 400-degree oven for 30 minutes. Remove the peppers from the oven. Peel off the portion of the skin that is loose. (Leave the skin that isn't loose on the peppers.) Reserve the peppers.

5. Boil or steam the fresh asparagus spears until they are tender but not mushy, about 5 to 7 minutes. Drain and set aside. (If you have a microwave oven, rinse the spears in cold water, shake the water off, spread the spears across a microwave dinner plate, and cover the plate tightly with plastic wrap. Set the plate in the microwave for 3 minutes on full power. Check the asparagus. If not done, cook the spears in the microwave for another 30 to 60 seconds, repeating the process until the spears are the right texture. Reserve.) If you're using frozen spears, follow the package directions for cooking and set aside.

6. Slice the mozzarella into pieces about ⅓ inch thick. Set aside.

FILLING

1 pound ricotta cheese

3 eggs, lightly beaten

2 tablespoons coarsely chopped Italian parsley

1¼ teaspoon coarsely ground black pepper

1 cup coarsely grated Romano or Parmesan cheese

½ cup (1 stick) butter

1 medium onion, peeled and sliced

2 cups fresh mushrooms, sliced

2 cups zucchini, sliced in ⅓-inch rounds

20 ounces (2 bags) fresh spinach (leaves and stems), washed, or 2 10-ounce packages frozen spinach

½ teaspoon garlic powder

1 teaspoon salt

¼ teaspoon crushed red pepper

2 red bell peppers, cored, halved, and seeded

2 yellow bell peppers, cored, halved and seeded

½ pound thin fresh asparagus spears or 1 package frozen asparagus spears, thawed

8 ounces (1 package) mozzarella cheese

1. Combine the butter and flour in a food processor fitted with the steel blade. Process until the dough pulls away from the side of the machine and forms a ball. (If this does not happen after about 45 seconds, then keep the machine running and add water, a tablespoon at a time, to the dough. Continue to process for another 30 seconds or so until a ball forms.)

2. Turn the dough out on a lightly floured surface. Divide the dough into a larger piece (about three-quarters of the total) and a smaller piece.

3. Roll out the larger piece of dough into a circle of dough 2 to 3 inches bigger than your 8-inch cakepan. Fit the circle of dough across the bottom and up the sides of the pan, piecing the dough together if you have to in order to cover the whole pan.

1. Spread about a third of the ricotta mixture across the dough in the cakepan. Then, working from the bottom up, layer the filling ingredients in the following order: the spinach, the red peppers (skin side up), another third of the ricotta mixture, the asparagus spears, the remaining third of the ricotta mixture, about half the mozzarella slices, the zucchini and mushrooms mixture, the rest of the mozzarella slices, and the yellow peppers (skin side up).

2. Roll out the remaining piece of dough to cover the filling. Place the dough on top of the torta. Pinch together the edges of both pieces of dough to seal the crust.

3. In a cup, mix together the egg and water and brush the top of the pie with this egg wash. With a paring knife, make four small slashes in the top crust to help steam to escape.

4. Bake the torta in a 350-degree oven for about an hour or until the top crust is lightly browned. (Check the progress after about 40 minutes.)

CRUST
1 cup (2 sticks) butter, cut in
1-inch pieces
2 cups flour
Water (if necessary)

ASSEMBLY
1 egg, lightly beaten
1 tablespoon water

PROSCIUTTO AND CHEESE PIE

Serves 16 as an appetizer, 6–8 as an entrée

This light yet delightfully filling pie, made with four different cheeses and a buttery crust, is rich, rich, rich. The Italians regard it as a specialty, eaten as a snack during the Easter holiday festivities. But I find the luscious prosciutto and cheese too good to resist the rest of the year and recommend it frequently to our customers as an hors d'oeuvre or as a good brunch or lunch food.

In a large bowl, using your hand or a fork, gently and thoroughly combine all the ingredients.

FILLING

1¹/4 *cups ricotta cheese*

¹/3 *pound smoked provolone cheese, diced small*

¹/2 *pound mozzarella cheese, diced small*

1²/3 *cups coarsely grated Parmesan cheese*

³/4 *cup (¹/4 pound) prosciutto (ask butcher to slice on #5 meat grinder), diced*

4 *eggs, beaten*

¹/4 *cup coarsely chopped Italian parsley*

1 *teaspoon coarsely ground black pepper*

1. Combine the flour and butter in a food processor fitted with the steel blade. Process until the dough pulls away from the side of the machine and forms a ball. (If this does not happen after about 45 seconds, keep the machine running and add 2 tablespoons of cold water to the dough. Continue to process for another 30 seconds or so until a ball forms.)

CRUST

3 *cups flour*

1 *cup (2 sticks) butter, cut into small pieces*

Water (if necessary)

2. Turn the dough out onto a lightly floured surface. Divide the dough in half. Roll out the two pieces of dough to fit a 9-inch cakepan, or a pretty baking plate of the same size that you can also use for serving.

3. Fit one round of dough along the bottom and up the sides of your pan or plate, letting any excess dough overlap the edge.

1. Fill the pie completely with the prosciutto and cheese mixture.

2. Place the other round of dough on top of the filled pie. Trim off the excess dough to give the pie a finished look. Set this excess dough aside for optional use (see below).

3. In a cup, mix together the eggs and water. Brush the top of the pie with this egg wash.

4. *Optional:* Roll the excess dough into thin, strip-like cords and arrange these cords along the top border of the pie. You can also cut flowers, hearts, or any design you like out of the excess dough. Paste your decorations to the top of the pie with another egg-and-water glaze.

5. Before setting it in the oven, pierce the top of the pie with a fork at least a dozen times to help steam to escape. Bake the pie in a 375-degree oven for 1 hour, or until the crust turns a lovely light brown. Let the pie cool for 30 minutes. Then, if necessary, transfer it to a serving plate; otherwise, serve immediately.

ASSEMBLY

2 eggs, lightly beaten

2 tablespoons water

SPINACH PIE

Serves 4–6

I fell in love with Rose Viola's spinach pie and with her son Cosmo about the same time. Rose, who became my mother-in-law a little while later, liked to serve this covered pie at the family's Christmas buffet table. Cosmo still likes to eat it.

1. Divide the dough in half. Roll out one half of the dough into a circle about ¼ inch thick and 11 inches in diameter. Fit the dough into a 10-inch pie plate, with an inch of dough overlapping the edge.

2. In a large bowl, combine the spinach, sliced olives, olive oil, garlic, anchovies, salt, and red pepper. Mix thoroughly. Then mound the mixture on top of the dough in the pie plate.

3. Roll out the other portion of dough into another 11-inch circle. Place this circle of dough over the filling. Press the top and bottom edges of the dough together to seal the pie.

4. Brush the top of the pie with oil and bake in a 400-degree oven for 30 minutes, or until golden brown.

2 pounds All-purpose Dough (see pp. 108–109)

20 ounces (2 packages) fresh spinach, washed

6 ounces (1 can) pitted black olives, sliced in quarters

¼ cup olive oil

3 garlic cloves, peeled and diced

1¾ ounces canned anchovies

¼ teaspoon salt

½ teaspoon crushed red pepper

Olive oil to brush the top crust

SQUID PIE

Serves 16 as an appetizer, 6 to 8 as an entrée

1. Place the squid in a large saucepan and add water to cover. Bring the water to a boil, lower the heat, and simmer for 1 hour. When the squid is done, drain and set aside to cool.

2. Meanwhile, in a large bowl, combine the parsley, garlic, tomatoes, salt, black pepper, and chopped green pepper. Mix well until thoroughly incorporated.

3. Cut the cooled squid into 1/2-inch pieces and add to the tomato mixture in the bowl. Mix well. Then place this mixture in a colander so that it drains thoroughly.

4. Roll out each pound of dough into a rectangle an inch larger than your cookie sheet. Lay one rectangle on the oiled sheet. (If it is difficult to move, gently fold it in quarters and move onto the cookie sheet. Then unfold.)

5. Pour the squid mixture over the dough on the cookie sheet. Cover the filling with the other rectangle of dough and seal by lifting the overlapping pieces of dough up over the edges of the cookie sheet to form a thick ridge.

6. Brush the top of the pizza with olive oil and make slits for steam to escape. Bake at 400 degrees for 30 minutes, or until golden brown.

5 pounds squid (cleaned), including tentacles

1 cup coarsely chopped Italian parsley

5 garlic cloves, peeled and minced

1 pound 12 ounces (1 can) whole peeled tomatoes, without juice

1 1/2 teaspoons salt

1/2 teaspoon coarsely ground black pepper

1 small green pepper, cored, seeded, and chopped fine

2 pounds All-purpose Dough (see pp. 108–109)

Olive oil to brush the top crust

CALZONE

Makes 3 individual calzone; serves 3–6

Calzone, the baked turnover originally from Naples, has also been called a mezzaluna, or half-moon, for its shape, and a folded pizza for its contents. No matter what you call it, once you've eaten a calzone you'll find it hard to return to an ordinary sandwich. Filled with meat, cheeses, or vegetables, a calzone is a meal in itself. Because they freeze and reheat beautifully, calzone are elegant enough for a party requiring advance preparation, and practical enough to make for yourself.

Here are the directions for shaping individual calzone. The recipes for calzone fillings follow separately.

1. Cut the pound of dough into three pieces. Roll out each piece into an oval about 8 inches long and 6 inches wide. It will be about ¼ inch thick.

2. Place the filling ingredients across the bottom center of each oval.

3. Fold each piece of dough in half over the filling to form three turnovers. Using the tines of a fork, pinch the edges of each calzone together to form a seal.

4. Mix the egg and water together in a small bowl or cup. Brush the top of the calzone with this egg wash. Then sprinkle poppy or sesame seeds generously on top of each calzone.

5. Place the calzone on an oiled cookie sheet and bake in a 400-degree oven for 30 minutes or until golden brown. Serve warm, room temperature, or cold.

NOTE: To make one large calzone, which will feed 12 people as an hors d'oeuvre, roll out the pound of dough into an oval measuring about 15 inches long and 10 inches wide and double the filling ingredients.

1 pound All-purpose Dough (see pp. 108–109)
Filling ingredients
1 egg, beaten
2 tablespoons water
Poppy seeds or sesame seeds
Oil for cookie sheet

When the filling ingredients are in place, lift one side of the dough over them and use the tines of a fork to crimp and seal the edges of the calzone.

ITALIAN CALZONE

1. Roll out the dough into three ovals, each about 8 inches long, 6 inches wide, and 1/4 inch thick.

2. Make three packets, each containing 3 slices mortadella, 4 slices salami, 2 slices peppered ham, 2 slices Swiss cheese, one tomato slice, and a round of onion cut in half.

3. Fold the dough in half over the filling and seal.

4. Mix the egg and water and brush the top of the calzone with the egg wash. Sprinkle with the seeds.

5. Bake the calzone on an oiled cookie sheet at 400 degrees for 30 minutes or until golden brown.

1 pound All-purpose Dough (see pp. 108–109)

1/8 pound mortadella, cut into 9 slices

1/8 pound Genoa salami, cut into 12 slices

1/8 pound Italian peppered ham or Danish ham, cut into 6 slices

1/8 pound Swiss cheese, cut into 6 slices

1 large tomato, sliced

1 medium onion (red or yellow), sliced in rounds 1/4 inch thick

1 egg, beaten

2 tablespoons water

Poppy seeds or sesame seeds

Oil for cookie sheet

VARIATION: This recipe works particularly well as a large calzone. To make a large one, roll the pound of dough into one big oval, about 15 inches long and 10 inches wide. Use the following ingredients for the filling with the cooking and baking instructions given above.

1/4 pound mortadella, sliced

1/4 pound salami, sliced

1/4 pound boiled ham, sliced

1/4 pound Swiss cheese, sliced

1/4 pound mozzarella cheese, sliced

3 tomatoes, sliced

1 large onion (red or yellow), sliced in rounds 1/4 inch thick

ZUCCHINI AND HERB CALZONE

Makes 3 individual calzone

1. Heat ¼ cup oil in a skillet over medium high heat. Add the vegetables, herbs, and seasonings and sauté until the vegetables are well done. Remove skillet from heat.

2. Roll out the dough into three ovals, each about 8 inches long, 6 inches wide, and ¼ inch thick.

3. Place a slice of mozzarella on each oval of dough. Cover each mozzarella slice with some of the sautéed vegetable mixture, then top with another slice of mozzarella and a slice of tomato, if you'd like.

4. Fold the dough in half over the filling and seal.

5. Mix the egg and water and brush the top of the calzone with the egg wash. Sprinkle with the seeds.

6. Bake the calzone on an oiled cookie sheet at 400 degrees for 30 minutes or until golden brown.

¼ cup oil

3 large zucchini, sliced into quarters, then into 1-inch pieces

1 large onion, peeled and sliced

2 garlic cloves, peeled and crushed

1 teaspoon dried thyme

1 teaspoon dried basil

1 teaspoon dried oregano

1 teaspoon coarsely ground black pepper

½ teaspoon salt

1 pound All-purpose Dough (see pp. 108–109)

6 slices mozzarella cheese

1 tomato, sliced (optional)

1 egg, beaten

2 tablespoons water

Poppy seeds or sesame seeds

Oil for cookie sheet

SAUSAGE CALZONE

1. Heat the 2 tablespoons oil in a skillet over medium high heat. Add the sausages and fry for about 15 minutes or until the sausages are half cooked. As the sausages brown in the skillet, cut them into small pieces and turn them often.

2. Add the sliced red, green, and yellow peppers and the onion to the skillet and cook thoroughly, 10 to 15 minutes. Remove from heat. Drain off all the liquid and set the mixture aside.

3. Roll out the dough into three ovals, each about 8 inches long, 6 inches wide, and ¼ inch thick.

4. Place a slice of mozzarella on top of each oval. Cover each mozzarella slice with some of the sausage mixture, then top with another slice of mozzarella.

5. Fold the dough in half over the filling and seal.

6. Mix the egg and water and brush the top of the calzone with the egg wash. Sprinkle with the seeds.

7. Bake the calzone on an oiled cookie sheet for 30 minutes, or until golden brown.

2 tablespoons oil

3 Italian sweet sausages (see p. 144 for homemade sweet sausages)

1 red bell pepper, cored, seeded, and sliced into thin strips

1 green bell pepper, cored, seeded, and sliced into thin strips

1 yellow bell pepper, cored, seeded, and sliced into thin strips

1 onion, peeled and sliced

1 pound All-purpose Dough (see pp. 108–109)

6 slices mozzarella cheese (whole or skim milk)

1 egg, beaten

2 tablespoons water

Poppy seeds or sesame seeds

Oil for cookie sheet

MASCARPONE AND OTHER CHEESE CALZONE

Makes 3 individual calzone

1. Combine the Cheddar, mozzarella, and provolone cheeses in a food processor fitted with the steel blade. Process coarsely and transfer to a mixing bowl.

2. Add the mascarpone and parsley to the cheeses in the bowl. Mix well with a spoon.

3. Roll out the dough into three ovals, each about 8 inches long, 6 inches wide, and 1/4 inch thick.

4. Fill the ovals with the cheese and parsley mixture.

5. Fold the dough in half over the filling and seal.

6. Mix the egg and water and brush the top of the calzone with the egg wash. Sprinkle with the seeds.

7. Bake the calzone on an oiled cookie sheet at 400 degrees for 30 minutes, or until golden brown.

1/3 pound Cheddar cheese
1/3 pound mozzarella cheese
1/2 pound provolone cheese
3 tablespoons mascarpone cheese
1/2 cup coarsely chopped Italian parsley
1 pound All-purpose Dough (see pp. 108–109)
1 egg, beaten
2 tablespoons water
Poppy seeds or sesame seeds
Oil for cookie sheet

TURKEY AND ASPARAGUS CALZONE

Makes 3 individual calzone

1. Roll out the dough into three ovals, each about 8 inches long, 6 inches wide, and 1/4 inch thick.

2. Place the asparagus spears in the Cheddar sauce. Coat each spear generously with the sauce.

3. Place 4 coated asparagus spears inside each slice of turkey breast. Roll up each turkey slice around the spears and arrange the rolled slices in the center of the ovals of dough.

4. Fold the dough in half over the filling and seal.

5. Mix the egg and water and brush the top of the calzone with the egg wash. Sprinkle with the seeds.

6. Bake the calzone on an oiled cookie sheet at 400 degrees for 30 minutes or until golden brown.

1. Melt the butter in a saucepan over medium high heat. Whisk in the flour and make a paste. Cook the paste for 1 minute.

2. Whisk in the cream, add the Cheddar cheese, and continue whisking until the cheese is all melted. Remove saucepan from heat.

3. Cool the sauce in the refrigerator until it is firm and cold so that it will adhere to the asparagus spears.

1 pound All-purpose Dough (see pp. 108–109)

12 fresh asparagus spears, cooked but still firm or 12 frozen spears, thawed but not cooked

Cheddar Sauce (see below)

3 slices turkey breast (sliced not too thin)

1 egg, beaten

2 tablespoons water

Poppy seeds or sesame seeds

Oil for cookie sheet

CHEDDAR SAUCE

4 tablespoons (1/2 stick) butter

2 tablespoons flour

1 cup heavy cream

1/4 pound Cheddar cheese, sliced or chopped

SUN-DRIED TOMATO, GOAT CHEESE, AND RICOTTA CALZONE

Makes 3 individual calzone

1. Place the sun-dried tomatoes in a food processor fitted with the steel blade. Process until coarsely chopped and transfer to a bowl.

2. Combine the ricotta and goat cheese in the food processor. Process briefly to incorporate them, and transfer to the bowl with the tomatoes.

3. Add the Parmesan, pine nuts, black pepper, and parsley to the mixture in the bowl. With a spoon, mix until well incorporated.

4. Roll out the dough into three ovals, each about 8 inches long, 6 inches wide, and ¼ inch thick.

5. Place one piece of mozzarella on top of each oval of dough. Cover the mozzarella with the filling, then top with another slice of mozzarella.

6. Fold the dough in half over the filling and seal.

7. Mix the egg and water and brush the top of the calzone with the egg wash. Sprinkle with the seeds.

8. Bake the calzone on an oiled cookie sheet at 400 degrees for 30 minutes, or until golden brown.

1 cup sun-dried tomatoes
1 pound ricotta cheese
6 ounces plain goat cheese
½ cup coarsely grated Parmesan cheese
3 tablespoons pine nuts
1 teaspoon coarsely ground black pepper
¼ cup coarsely chopped Italian parsley
1 pound All-purpose Dough (see pp. 108–109)
6 slices mozzarella cheese
1 egg, beaten
2 tablespoons water
Poppy seeds or sesame seeds
Oil for cookie sheet

SAUSAGES

HOMEMADE SAUSAGES
* Sweet Italian Fennel
* Hot Fennel
* Basil Pine Nut
* Garlic
PATES
* Pate de Campagna
* Pate de Legumes
* Mousse Truffee
* Mousse Royale
* Pate de Canards
                    L'Orange
* Pate Maison

O ONE COULD BE MORE THRIFTY THAN AN ITALIAN with a hog. In the households where each of my parents grew up, the wives would raise the pigs, the husbands butcher them, and the entire family would live off the homemade pork products. The pigs' feet were preserved in gelatin or browned and, along with the hocks, used in stews. Pancetta, or Italian bacon, was made by seasoning the pork belly with spices and salt and curing it. Pressed in salt and water with heavy weights, the shoulder, or ham, became prosciutto. The guts became the casings for salami. The loins, of course, were fried as pork chops and the rendered fat, or lard, was used as shortening. Even the tail was cooked, providing flavor for red sauce. And the pig's head was baked whole until the meat fell off the bone. They used practically every inch of every hog; nothing was wasted. And the most valued parts of all were the pig's lungs and liver, because these were the pieces of pork that became sausages.

To make the sausages, the liver and lungs were ground together and mixed with salt, cracked pepper, and often a little fennel. This meat was then stuffed into its own natural casings, the cleaned intestines of the same slaughtered pig. Italian families hung these sausages to dry down in their cool, dark cellars. Without benefit of refrigeration, the sausages were left to dry there for a month, sometimes even longer.

Like my parents, my husband Cosmo grew up eating such home-grown sausages, on the last farm in the city of Somerville, Massachusetts. Neapolitan families like the Cremaldis had long relied on their hogs to provide them with food and more. In fact, Naples was probably the last important Western city in which each household used its own pig to clean the surrounding street. I, meanwhile, never even got to taste, much less prepare, the kind of fresh pork that sustained my parents and husband, not to mention European peasants and American pioneers for centuries. Several years before I was born in Republic, Pennsylvania, an ordinance was passed prohibiting the raising of hogs within town limits.

Maybe, had I cleaned and dried my own pork, I might have felt differently about sausages. Certainly I always thought they were very beautiful to look at in their casings and smelled heavenly when fried. But I've also found most sausages simply too fatty and too salty for my taste. And so, a few years ago, I started grinding fresh pork shoulder without any fat and using next to no salt, making sausages myself. I made the traditional hot sausage hotter by adding more pepper; the traditional sweet sausage I made sweeter with an extra pinch of fennel. And then I really began to experiment with sausages, as I had with macaroni, mixing and matching flavors within the casings.

Since that time I've been surprised at how few cookbooks offer sausage recipes. Although it's usually considered complex and even a bit mysterious, the preparation is really quite easy. To begin, all you'll need is a pastry bag fitted with a long nozzle—or, better yet, make an investment in a hand meat grinder with a long nozzle, also known as a stuffing horn attachment. I don't really recommend using a food processor to grind meat for sausage, as the results are too finely ground. If you don't have a meat grinder, ask your butcher to grind the meat to the right consistency for sausage.

The recipes in this chapter all follow the simple procedure below. But if you'd prefer not to use casings or purchase a meat grinder, or if the equipment is unavailable, you can still enjoy the fillings. Just shape and fry your sausage as a patty. As you're about to discover, a sausage can come in many guises; it doesn't even have to include pork, unless, of course, you are lucky enough to be raising your own hog. ◆

SAUSAGES

1. Prepare the filling and set aside.

2. Place the casing in a bowl of warm water in your kitchen sink. It will relax nearly instantly. Meanwhile, set up the sausage grinder with the long nozzle (stuffing horn) attachment, following the manufacturer's instructions.

3. Take the casing out of the water and fit the open end over the sink's faucet. Turn on the warm water gently to allow the water to run through the casing. Then remove the end of the casing from the faucet and immediately slide the end over the sausage nozzle.

4. Place the filling in the top of the grinder and crank the machine so that the filling feeds into the casing. Continue cranking until the entire casing is filled.

5. *To link:* Using the butcher's twine, tie a knot every 4 inches along the length of the sausage.

6. *To cook:* Fry the sausages in a little oil, turning them frequently. After about 25 minutes, they should be browned, crispy, and ready to serve. Or place the sausages in a shallow pan and bake them in a 375-degree oven for about 45 minutes, turning them occasionally. Or barbecue the sausages on an outdoor grill to enjoy my favorite way of eating them.

Filling ingredients

7-foot-long natural hog casing (available as special order from most butchers)

2 yards butcher's twine

SWEET ITALIAN FENNEL SAUSAGE

Serves 6–8

When a particular flavor is supposed to predominate, why not use it in abundance? It's the extra fennel that makes my sweet sausage sweeter, and tastier, than those I ate as a child.

In a large mixing bowl, using your hand or a fork, combine all the ingredients for the filling. Prepare the casing (see recipe for Sausages), fill, link, and cook.

2 pounds coarsely ground pork shoulder

1 teaspoon coarsely ground black pepper

2 teaspoons salt

1 heaping tablespoon whole fennel seed

1 tablespoon ground fennel

2 tablespoons white wine

1/2 cup coarsely chopped Italian parsley

7-foot-long natural casing

2 yards butcher's twine

HOT ITALIAN FENNEL SAUSAGE

Serves 6–8

I am lavish with the red pepper in my version of the traditional hot sausage. Maybe that's what makes it so popular. People know that sometimes you just can't get enough of a good thing.

In a large mixing bowl, using your hand or a fork, combine all the ingredients for the filling. Prepare the casing (see recipe for Sausages), fill, link, and cook.

2 pounds coarsely ground pork shoulder

1 teaspoon coarsely ground black pepper

2 teaspoons salt

1 heaping tablespoon whole fennel seed

1 tablespoon ground fennel

2 tablespoons white wine

1 cup coarsely chopped Italian parsley

1 tablespoon crushed red pepper

7-foot-long natural casing

2 yards butcher's twine

PROVOLONE SAUSAGE

Serves 6–8

When I was growing up, my family melted cheese inside and on top of just about everything from bread to dessert. But we never thought to fill a sausage with cheese. I'm awfully glad Ricco DiCenzo, who works at Andy's Meat Market in Boston's North End, did.

In a large mixing bowl, using your hand or a fork, combine all the ingredients for the filling. Prepare the casing (see recipe for Sausages), fill, link, and cook.

2 pounds coarsely ground pork shoulder

3/4 pound (3 cups) sharp provolone cheese, diced by hand in small pieces

1 heaping tablespoon coarsely ground black pepper

1 teaspoon salt

7-foot-long natural casing

2 yards butcher's twine

BASIL-PINE NUT SAUSAGE

Serves 6–8

I invented this recipe during my search for a leaner, less salty version of the sausages I had eaten as a child. What I ended up creating wasn't a traditional Italian pork sausage at all, but one that is as delicious as it is original. It's enjoyable any time, and I especially love serving Basil-Pine Nut Sausage at a big country breakfast.

In a large mixing bowl, using your hand or a fork, combine all the ingredients for the filling. Prepare the casing (see recipe for Sausages), fill, link, and cook.

2 pounds coarsely ground pork shoulder

3/4 cup Pesto Sauce (see p. 75)

1 cup coarsely grated Romano cheese

1 bunch coarsely chopped Italian parsley

1/2 cup whole pine nuts

6 large garlic cloves, peeled and chopped

1 tablespoon coarsely ground black pepper

7-foot-long natural casing

2 yards butcher's twine

PEPPERONI AND CHICKEN SAUSAGE

Serves 6–8

Sausages are usually thought of as in-house fare, appropriate for a family brunch or a Sunday night supper but rarely served to company. Reputations are slow to change, of course. But making this wonderful sausage might change your mind.

1. Place the chicken breasts in a food processor fitted with the steel blade. Process briefly, until chicken has the consistency of sausage meat. Then transfer to a bowl.

2. Cut the pepperoni in 1-inch chunks. Process until fine and combine with chicken in the bowl.

3. Place the peppers in the food processor. Process until peppers are diced. Using a piece of cheesecloth, if you have it, or just your hands, squeeze the juice out of the peppers. Then add them to the bowl.

1 1/2 pounds boneless, skinless chicken breasts

1 stick pepperoni with outer casing removed

1/2 red, 1/2 yellow, and 1/2 green bell pepper, cored and seeded

2 tablespoons white wine

1 teaspoon salt

4. Add the wine, salt, parsley, and cheese to the filling. Mix well by hand.

5. Prepare the casing (see recipe for Sausages), fill, link, and cook.

1/2 cup coarsely chopped Italian parsley

1/2 cup coarsely grated Locatelli or Romano cheese

7-foot-long natural casing

2 yards butcher's twine

CORIANDER SAUSAGE

Serves 6–8

Like the Cremaldis, the Amendola family emigrated from the area around Naples known as Gaeta and settled in what was then the predominantly Italian section of Somerville and East Cambridge. There Anna Amendola opened a little store in which she made homemade sausages. Often she would sell as much as eighty pounds a week. This Coriander Sausage, Anna says, was a particular favorite of her customers.

In a large mixing bowl, using your hand or a fork, combine all the ingredients for the filling. Prepare the casing (see recipe for Sausages), fill, link, and cook.

2 pounds coarsely ground pork shoulder

2 tablespoons whole coriander seeds

1 tablespoon ground coriander

1 cup chopped fresh cilantro

1 teaspoon coarsely ground black pepper

1/2 teaspoon crushed red pepper

2 teaspoons salt

7-foot-long natural casing

2 yards butcher's twine

GARLIC SAUSAGE

Serves 6–8

The chunks of garlic, visible inside the casing, make this sausage appealing to the eye as well as to the palate.

In a large mixing bowl, using your hands or a fork, combine all the ingredients for the filling. Prepare the casing (see recipe for Sausages), fill, link, and cook.

2 pounds coarsely ground pork shoulder

2 teaspoons salt

1 teaspoon coarsely ground black pepper

1 teaspoon garlic powder

8 large garlic cloves, peeled and coarsely chopped

7-foot-long natural casing

2 yards butcher's twine

VEAL AND SAGE SAUSAGE

Serves 6–8

Like rosemary and chicken, veal and sage just seem to go together. This sausage is one delicious product of their union.

In a large mixing bowl, using your hand or a fork, combine all the ingredients for the filling. Prepare the casing (see recipe for Sausages), fill, link, and cook.

2 pounds veal fillet coarsely ground

1 tablespoon rubbed sage

2 teaspoons salt

1 teaspoon coarsely ground black pepper

7-foot-long natural casing

2 yards butcher's twine

ORANGE-SPICE SAUSAGE

Serves 6–8

No doubt you've sipped orange-spice tea and maybe even savored a fruit-stuffed loin of pork. So why not try Orange-Spice Sausage?

1. With a cheese grater, grate the peel of the orange fairly fine.

2. In a large mixing bowl, using your hand or a fork, combine all the ingredients for the filling. Prepare the casing (see recipe for Sausages), fill, link, and cook.

1 *large orange, for peel*

2 *pounds coarsely ground pork shoulder*

1/2 *teaspoon allspice*

1/2 *teaspoon cloves*

1/2 *teaspoon cumin*

1/2 *teaspoon cayenne pepper*

1/2 *teaspoon ground fennel*

1/2 *teaspoon cinnamon*

2 *teaspoons salt*

7-foot-long natural casing

2 *yards butcher's twine*

GARLIC

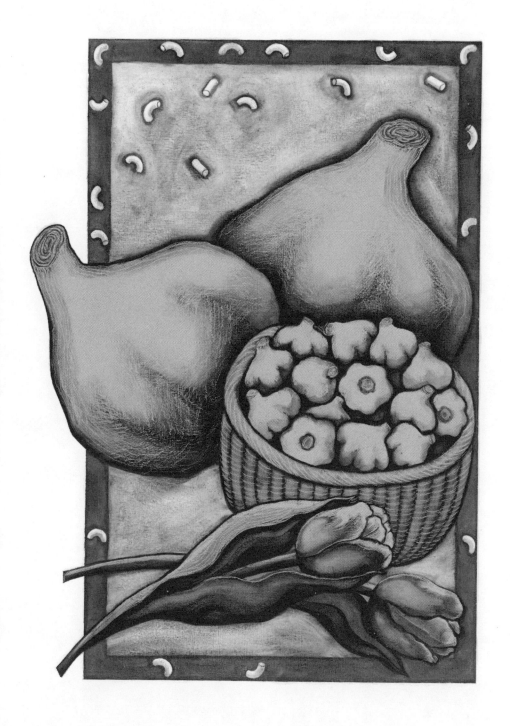

I HAVE ALWAYS HAD AN ALMOST MYSTICAL ATTRACTION TO GARlic. Even as a child, I was fascinated by the garlic growing in my grandparents' garden. Every spring I would start to imagine those silky bulbs still hidden under the ground; my mouth would burn to bite into one of the fresh raw cloves. Armed with only a stick, I would get down on my hands and knees in the dirt between the rows of vegetables. Even before the green, scallion-like leaves shot up through the soil, I would dig. To this day, I'll never know why it was so easy for me to find the garlic several inches deep in mud. It was as though the loot were lying in wait and I had somehow been led to the exact spot where I could unearth the buried treasure.

Of course, I wasn't the first person to fall under garlic's special spell. Homer's Odysseus used garlic as a charm protecting him against the sorcerer Circe. The ancient Greeks apparently believed that garlic endowed them with physical strength: their athletes chewed it when competing in Olympic games; their soldiers ate it before going into battle. In the Middle Ages, people wore garlic necklaces to ward off vampires. And in more recent times practitioners of folk medicine have recommended doses of garlic to cure everything from worms to whooping cough.

While garlic can exert a powerful influence, in cooking its true nature has remained elusive. After all, what other food changes flavor so dramatically depending on whether it's crushed or eaten whole? Technically, garlic, whose botanical name is *Allium sativum,* is a vegetable belonging to the onion family. But most people think of garlic—peeled, minced, and frequently fried—primarily as a seasoning. To do so is to miss out on a great opportunity. While garlic plays a nice supporting role in the preparation of many dishes, when the garlic taste is allowed to predominate—in a soup or a roast, for instance—the ultimate flavor can be even better. And strangely enough, sometimes the more garlic you use, the less you can tell you're eating it. Besides, garlic is good for you.

Regardless of the amount called for, garlic is the most important ingredient in all of the recipes in this chapter. You can cook with any fresh garlic that has either a creamy white or a purplish cast or the larger elephant garlic, if you prefer, which has a milder flavor. The heads should be plump and firm to the touch when you buy them and stored in a cool, dry place to preserve their freshness. My mother used to braid her garlic and hang it from the ceiling; some people successfully keep theirs in the refrigerator, separated from the other vegetables; I leave my garlic in a bowl on a counter top or sometimes in the freezer. When it comes to peeling the garlic, I've never approved of the kitchen-knife method that's usually recommended. Instead, I strike the individual cloves lightly but sharply with a hammer or a mallet and find the papery skins come off instantly.

Even after it's cooked and consumed, garlic continues to have an effect. If I rub half a lemon over my fingers, I can eliminate the garlic smell there, but no matter how much parsley I chew, my husband Cosmo can always detect the pungent odor on my breath. Garlic gets into your clothes, into your pores, into your system itself. This strange vegetable ends up everywhere. Maybe that explains garlic's enduring power. ◆

ROASTED GARLIC

Serves 4–8

These wonderful morsels of garlic make an unbeatable appetizer. To serve them, Laura, who cooks for Cremaldi's, suggests starting with chunks or small slices of Italian bread. Spread each piece of bread with goat cheese, squeeze the garlic over the cheese, and top with a sliver of sun-dried tomatoes. It will be a tough act to follow.

1. With a serrated knife, cut across the top of each head of garlic, exposing about 1/4 of an inch of each clove.

2. Set the heads of garlic in a small cakepan. Pour the olive oil over the heads and sprinkle them with the pepper.

3. Roast the garlic in a 450-degree oven for 45 minutes. The garlic will cool relatively quickly; to serve, separate the cloves and enjoy this delectable spread.

4 large heads garlic, unpeeled
1/2 cup olive oil
1 teaspoon coarsely ground black pepper

ROASTED RED PEPPERS, ANCHOVY, AND GARLIC

Serves 4–6 as lunch; 10–12 as appetizer

There's nothing timid about the flavors in this dish that join forces to make a memorable midday meal or first course. Don't be afraid to really char the peppers either; they'll be easier to peel if you get them good and black.

1. Place the peppers under a broiler or hold them on a long fork over an open gas flame. Turn them as they char, until their surfaces are completely black. This should take about 10 minutes.

2. Transfer the charred peppers to a closed container and let them "sweat" for 20 minutes.

3. Peel off the charred skin of each pepper. (The flesh will still be red underneath.) Then cut the stems off the peppers, halve them, and remove the seeds.

4. Place the pepper halves on your serving platter. Arrange 2 anchovy fillets across the top of each pepper half.

5. Mix the oil and minced garlic together in a bowl. Pour the mixture over the peppers and anchovies and serve at room temperature to bring out the full flavor.

6 large red bell peppers, left whole
24 anchovy fillets
1 cup olive oil
6 large garlic cloves, peeled and minced

TOASTER OVEN GARLIC BREAD

Serves 6–8

I think it was the French who first had the tasty idea of rubbing toasted bread with garlic before buttering it. It's a fast, practical, and easy way to make garlic bread. The dry toast acts as a grater and gathers a good amount of flavor before it's drizzled with oil or brushed with butter.

1. Cut bread into slices about 1 inch thick, or to your liking. Toast the slices.

2. Rub the pieces of toast with the garlic cloves.

3. Drizzle each piece of toast with a little olive oil (or brush each piece with a little butter) and serve immediately.

1 loaf Italian or Tuscan bread
4 garlic cloves, peeled
Olive oil or butter

GARLIC-BASIL BREAD

Serves 4–6

1. In a food processor fitted with the steel blade, combine the basil leaves, oil, garlic, both cheeses, and black pepper. Process until fine.

2. Melt the butter in a skillet over medium high heat. Add the basil mixture and cook for 3 to 5 minutes.

3. Slice the bread. Brush both sides of each slice of bread with the cooked basil mixture.

4. Arrange the brushed bread on a cookie sheet. Broil the slices for 3 minutes on each side.

1 cup fresh basil leaves, including the tender part of the stems, loosely packed in measuring cup

1/2 cup oil

8 garlic cloves, peeled

2 tablespoons coarsely grated Parmesan cheese

2 tablespoons coarsely grated Romano cheese

1 teaspoon coarsely ground black pepper

1/2 cup (1 stick) butter

1 loaf Tuscan or Italian bread

STRONG GARLIC-BALSAMIC DRESSING

Makes about 3 cups dressing

The taste of balsamic vinegar has always reminded me of the bottom of my grandfather's wine barrel. Frankly, I'm usually not all that wild about this vinegar which begins as sweet white grape juice and takes years, if not generations, to age. Still, it's one of the few flavors strong enough to stand up to garlic. The result is not only an unusual combination, it's also a wonderfully aromatic and powerful dressing that's especially good when served over a salad of lettuce, red and yellow peppers, cucumbers, and carrot rounds, or over artichoke hearts.

1. Purée the garlic in a food processor fitted with the steel blade.

2. Add all the other ingredients and purée them, along with the garlic, for 15 seconds.

1 cup garlic cloves, peeled

1 1/2 cups olive oil

1 cup balsamic vinegar

1 teaspoon coarsely ground black pepper

10 fresh basil leaves

2 teaspoons salt

3 1/2 ounces (1 container) mascarpone cheese

2 teaspoons sugar

LAURA'S GARLIC SOUP

Hearty, thick, rich, this main-course soup is surprisingly easy to make. The other surprising thing about this soup is that the longer it sits out, the more intense the garlic flavor gets.

1. Divide the garlic heads into cloves and peel them.

2. In a large pot with at least a 6-quart capacity, combine all the ingredients including the bread and white wine.

3. Bring the soup to a boil over high heat. Then reduce heat to a simmer. Cook uncovered for 1 hour, stirring occasionally.

4. When the soup is cooked, purée it in batches in a blender or food processor and serve.

2 large heads garlic

1 quart chicken stock (canned is fine)

1 quart beef stock (canned is fine)

1 heaping tablespoon ground coriander

1 tablespoon paprika, preferably hot

1/2 teaspoon salt

1/2 teaspoon white pepper

1/2 loaf day-old French or Tuscan bread, torn into chunks

1 cup dry white wine

BAGNO CALDO

Makes enough sauce for 1–1½ pounds macaroni

It seems that every Italian cook has his or her own version of the traditional "hot bath." This version belongs to Rosie, who cooks for Cremaldi's. She likes to serve it over spaghetti. It's one of the most delicious sauces I know.

1. Heat the oil in a skillet over medium high heat. Sauté the garlic and the anchovies together in the oil, mashing the anchovies as you fry them. Sprinkle in the black pepper. Cook until some of the garlic cloves are brown.

2. Add the water slowly. (Don't worry about the oil splattering.) Cook for 3 more minutes.

3. Mix in the raisins and the nut pieces. Cook for 3 additional minutes. Serve hot over macaroni.

1½ cups olive oil

1/2 cup peeled garlic cloves

1 jar (3.17 ounces) anchovies

1 teaspoon coarsely ground black pepper

2 tablespoons water

1/2 cup raisins

1/2 cup walnut pieces

MILANESE GARLIC SOUP

People will have a hard time guessing the ingredients in this soup. The garlic takes on an intriguingly different flavor, and the chopped vegetables here seem just to disappear. But whether or not you reveal this recipe, there's one thing your guests will know for sure. This soup is so smooth and rich they'll be eager to come back for more.

1. In a food processor fitted with the steel blade, combine the carrots, celery, onion, and garlic. Process briefly, until the ingredients are finely chopped.

2. Melt half the stick of butter in a saucepan or deep skillet over medium high heat. Add the chopped vegetables, along with the coriander, and sauté for about 10 minutes, until tender.

3. Pour the sherry into the vegetable mixture and simmer for a few minutes. Then pour in the chicken stock and simmer for 20 more minutes, whisking on occasion.

4. Meanwhile, knead together the other half stick of butter and the flour into a soft ball.

5. Raise the heat underneath the vegetables. Gently break the butter-and-flour ball into small pieces and whisk each piece into the vegetable mixture until thoroughly incorporated. Reduce the heat to a low rolling boil and simmer the soup for 10 minutes, stirring on occasion.

6. Whisk in the heavy cream and serve immediately, steaming hot.

2 carrots, peeled and cut into chunks

2 celery stalks, trimmed and cut into pieces

1 medium yellow onion, peeled and quartered

20 large garlic cloves or 40 small cloves, peeled

1/2 cup (1 stick) butter

1 heaping teaspoon ground coriander

1/4 cup sherry

1 quart chicken stock (canned or homemade)

1/4 cup flour

1/2 cup heavy cream

GARLIC PIE

Like a covered pizza with a flakier crust, this tasty pie is ideal for lunch, an hors d'oeuvre, or a snack. Maybe because the cloves are left whole or, paradoxically, because there are so many of them, the pie's main ingredient may even go undetected.

1. Melt the butter for the filling in a skillet over medium high heat. Add the garlic cloves and sugar and sauté, stirring often, for 15 minutes. Meanwhile, prepare the crust.

2. In a food processor fitted with a steel blade, combine the butter and flour for the crust. Process until the dough forms a ball. (If it does not form a ball in 20 seconds, add water, a tablespoon at a time, and continue to run the processor until a ball forms.)

3. Place this ball of dough on your work surface and divide it in half. Roll out each piece of dough into a circle about half an inch larger than a cakepan measuring 6 inches in diameter and 2 inches in depth. Fit one circle of dough across the bottom and up the sides of the pan. Leave about 1/2 inch of dough overlapping the pan's edge.

4. Fold each slice of provolone in half and place the folded slices on top of the dough in the pan. Cover the provolone with the sautéed garlic mixture. Then fold the slices of Swiss cheese in half and place them over the garlic.

5. Cover the pie with the other circle of dough. Trim off the excess dough around the edge.

6. Mix the egg and water together in a small bowl or cup. Brush the top of the pie with this egg wash. Bake the pie in a 400-degree oven for 30 minutes or longer, until it is golden brown.

FILLING

1/2 *cup (1 stick) butter*
 3 *cups peeled whole garlic cloves*
1 1/2 *tablespoons sugar*
 6 *slices provolone cheese*
 6 *slices Swiss cheese*

CRUST

1/2 *cup (1 stick) butter, cut into chunks*
 2 *cups flour*
 1 *egg, beaten*
 2 *tablespoons water*

GARLIC PIZZA

Makes 1 large pizza; serves 4–6

The flavor of garlic is in the shadows of many pizza toppings. Here's garlic's chance, in this familiar thick and crusty setting, to have its moment in the sun.

1. Roll out the dough into a rectangle about an inch longer and an inch wider than a jelly-roll pan measuring 17¼ × 11½ × 1 inches. Oil the pan. Fit the dough across the pan, leaving about an inch of dough overlapping the edges. With your fingers, lift and roll the overlapping dough up over the edges of the pan to form a thick ridge.

2. Line the dough with the American cheese and then the mozzarella.

3. Using your hands, squash the tomatoes over the whole pizza. Add the minced garlic, making sure it covers the surface.

4. Sprinkle on the pepper, oregano, and grated Romano. Bake the pizza in a 400-degree oven for 30 minutes or until golden brown.

1 pound All-purpose Dough (see pp. 108–109)

Oil for pan

12 slices American cheese

12 slices mozzarella cheese

1 pound 12 ounces (1 can) whole peeled tomatoes, without juice

20 garlic cloves, peeled and minced

2 teaspoons coarsely ground black pepper

2 teaspoons dried oregano

2 cups coarsely grated Romano cheese

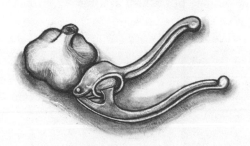

PORK WITH GARLIC AND POTATOES

This was the only way we ever had pork loin when I was growing up. It was good then; it still is.

1. With a paring knife, make ten slits, each as wide as the knife, in the pork loin. Stagger the placement of the slits over the whole roast. Insert a clove of garlic into each slit.

2. Sprinkle the salt, pepper, and rosemary over the pork. Cover the pork with the chunks of butter.

3. Pour the cup of water into the bottom of a roasting pan. Set the pork in the pan and roast, uncovered, in a 400-degree oven for 1 hour.

4. After an hour, place the potato pieces all around the roast. Salt and pepper the potatoes and add more water to the bottom of the pan, if it's dry. Continue to cook for 1½ hours longer, turning the potatoes a couple of times.

5-pound boned pork loin (ask butcher to tie it up)

10 garlic cloves, peeled and left whole

2 teaspoons salt, plus a sprinkling for potatoes

1 tablespoon coarsely ground black pepper, plus a sprinkling for potatoes

1/4 cup dried rosemary leaves

1/2 cup (1 stick) butter, cut in chunks

1 cup water

3 sweet potatoes and 3 large white potatoes, peeled and cut in 2-inch pieces

SOUPS AND STEWS

BACK IN REPUBLIC, PENNSYLVANIA, MY MOTHER NEVER made a soup without a shinbone. Not just any shinbone would do, of course. It had to be one rich in marrow with a lot of meat still on the bone. Boiling that bone in a pot filled with water, carrots, celery, and onions—the noodles were cooked separately and added later—was all my mother needed to do to produce her savory broth. Usually she bought a shinbone with soup in mind. But sometimes my mother would send my cousin Kiki and me through the thick woods to board the trolley, straight out of an old cartoon, and ride, with the breeze blowing in our faces, to the company store.

To outside observers it was a large, nondescript brick building that looked like a mill; for the coal miners, like my father, it was a monopolistic trap—the only place for miles where they could buy on credit. But for Kiki and me the company store was wonderful, a little paradise where our fantasies knew no bounds. For inside the store's huge expanse there weren't just meats, grains, and all the other basics every miner's family needed. There was also candy, jewelry, shoes, and a perfume counter that sold Evening in Paris cologne. In its beautiful cobalt blue bottle with the tassle, Evening in Paris was Kiki's and my ultimate luxury item. After going to the butcher, while waiting for the trolley back, we doused ourselves with the stuff and tried to forget that we were just two little girls who had been sent by my mother to buy a shinbone.

Whenever I cook soup, it stirs up memories of these trips from the simple to the sublime. Americans have long regarded soups and stews in a similar way, as both humble and elegant food. During the late eighteenth and most of the nineteenth century, soup was given to soldiers, prisoners, and saloon patrons as a free lunch; at the same time, the nation's finest restaurants were serving consommés and cream soups to those who could afford them. Meanwhile, the majority of Americans in this period ignored the dish entirely. Not until the turn of the century did people begin to recognize soup's nutritional and economic virtues.

And it wasn't until I moved to Cambridge, Massachusetts, at the age of fourteen, that I began to appreciate how much the beauty of a soup or stew is in the eye of the beholder. There I was in a fancy French restaurant, in the middle of academia, trying to decipher the menu and decide what to order. "Purée," "potage," and "velouté"—none of the soups, so strange and exotic-sounding, seemed to bear any resemblance to the hearty, homey broths I had known. When the waiter came, I bravely pointed to the word vichyssoise, to me the most foreign and fascinating soup name of all. During the few minutes it took for my vichyssoise to arrive, I began to regret my bold move. You can imagine my amazement and my relief, then, when the bowl set in front of me turned out to be filled with a soup that looked like, smelled like, and even tasted like my father's potato and onion. The only difference was that this one was cold! ◆

MY MOTHER'S SIMPLE CHICK-PEA AND MACARONI SOUP

This good soup is simple for more reasons than one. Not only is it easy to cook, but it's what my mother would make when she had leftover spaghetti sauce and a few slices of bacon and not much else in the house.

1. Bring the water to a boil in a large pot. Meanwhile, fry the bacon in a deep skillet.

2. When the bacon is cooked, drain off the fat and return the bacon to the skillet. Add the tomato sauce and the drained chick-peas to the bacon and let simmer together over very low heat for about 10 minutes.

3. Drop the ditalini in the boiling water and cook until done, about 2 minutes. When the ditalini are cooked, add the sauce mixture from the skillet to the pot of water with the pasta. Stir. Let soup continue to simmer in the pot for 15 minutes more. Serve, topped with grated cheese if you'd like.

VARIATION: If you don't have Famous Tomato Sauce in your refrigerator or freezer, you can improvise by using a small skillet or saucepan to make the following sauce:

1. Heat the oil in the skillet or saucepan over medium high heat. Add the crushed garlic and sauté for 5 minutes.

2. Add the tomato paste, water, basil, salt, sugar, and black pepper to the sautéed garlic.

3. Combine the sauce with the fried bacon and drained chickpeas in the skillet and continue to make the soup according to the directions above.

4 quarts water

1/2 pound bacon, cut in 1-inch pieces

1 cup Famous Tomato Sauce (see p. 69 or VARIATION below)

1 can (1 pound 4 ounces) chick-peas, drained

1 pound ditalini

Romano cheese, coarsely grated (optional)

1/4 cup oil

4 garlic cloves, peeled and crushed

6 ounces (1 can) tomato paste

1 tomato paste can of water

1/2 teaspoon dried basil

1 teaspoon salt

1/2 teaspoon sugar

1/2 teaspoon coarsely ground black pepper

POOR MAN'S SOUP

Serves 4–6

This simple soup is the one my grandmother cooked to revive stale bread. It will perk up your spirits, too.

1. Pour the water and the broth into a very large soup pot (at least a 6-quart capacity). Add the scallions and the potatoes. Season with the pepper and salt. Stir. Cook, uncovered, over medium high heat for at least 1 hour, until the potatoes are tender.

2. To serve, tear off chunks of hard Italian bread, a day or two old, and drop them into a soup tureen or individual soup bowls. Ladle in the soup and sprinkle the top with coarsely grated Romano cheese.

1 quart water

46 ounces (1 quart, 14-ounce can) chicken broth

2 bunches scallions, cut in 2-inch pieces

5 large potatoes, peeled and cut in 1/2-inch slices

1 tablespoon coarsely ground black pepper

Salt

Hard Italian bread

Romano cheese, coarsely grated

LENTIL SOUP

Serves 4–6

Because meat wasn't plentiful when I was a child, my family made whatever soups they could with water rather than beef stock. Now I wouldn't think of cooking lentil soup any other way. It's a wonderful, and wonderfully easy to prepare, vegetarian meal.

Put all the ingredients into a large pot and simmer for 1 hour and 15 minutes.

1 pound lentils

12 cups water

1 large carrot, scraped and sliced in 1/2-inch rounds

2 celery stalks, including leaves, cut in 3-inch pieces

1 large onion, peeled and sliced

2 tablespoons salt

1 teaspoon coarsely ground black pepper

2 tablespoons olive oil

DAD'S PEA SOUP

Nothing could be more nourishing, satisfying, or easier to make for your family on a cold winter's night than this country-style pea soup.

1. Combine all the ingredients except the ditalini in a large soup pot. Bring to a boil, lower the heat, and simmer for 2 hours.

2. In a separate pot, cook the ditalini according to the package directions. Drain well and add to the soup.

8 *cups water*

4 *cups dried split peas*

3/4 *pound Cotechino sausage, cut in 1-inch chunks, or 2 ham hocks, weighing up to 3/4 pound*

2 *carrots, scraped and cut in 1/2-inch slices*

3 *celery stalks, including leaves, cut in 1/4-inch chunks*

1/2 *medium onion, peeled and sliced*

2 *tablespoons olive oil*

1 *teaspoon salt*

1 *heaping teaspoon coarsely ground black pepper*

1/2 *cup ditalini (or any other small macaroni)*

BEANS AND MACARONI

With the red sauce left over from our Sunday dinner and fresh eggs for the fettucine coming from our own chicken coop, Pasta e Fagioli, as this dish is called in Italian, was one of the easiest and most economical meals for my mother to make. The red sauce has to be made from scratch and the eggs bought at the store, but beans and macaroni is still a satisfying and convenient dish to make today.

1. Bring the 8 cups of water to a boil in a large soup pot. Meanwhile, prepare the sauce.

2. Heat the oil in a skillet over medium high heat. Sauté the garlic in the oil until the cloves are slightly brown. Add the tomatoes, breaking them up with a spoon, along with the basil, 1 teaspoon of salt, and the pepper. Simmer the sauce for about 15 minutes while you cook the fettucine.

3. When the water is boiling, drop in the homemade fettucine and stir. (If you're using packaged fettucine, follow directions to cook al dente.) When the water returns to a boil, cook the fettucine for 2 minutes. Leave the cooked fettucine in the pot with the water, which should look starchy.

4. Pour the sauce into the same pot as the fettucine and water. Add the kidney beans and the other teaspoon of salt and remove from heat. Ladle into soup bowls, sprinkle with Romano cheese, and serve.

8 cups water

1/4 cup oil

2 large garlic cloves, peeled and crushed

2 cups canned whole tomatoes, without juice

1 teaspoon dried basil or 1 tablespoon finely chopped fresh basil

2 teaspoons salt

1 teaspoon coarsely ground black pepper

1 pound fettucine (preferably homemade), cut in 3-inch pieces

1 pound, 4 ounces (1 can) red kidney beans, drained

Coarsely grated Romano cheese

KALE STEW

Kale hasn't always been so popular, but when I was a child this green and the potatoes were the only parts of my father's stew that I would eat. After a while, I started nibbling the meaty portions of the pork hocks and finally I learned to savor the fat off the bones. It tastes as good, if not better than, the vegetables and the meat.

1. Heat the oil in a large Dutch oven or a shallow saucepan over medium high heat. Add the garlic and the pork hocks or pigs' feet, and fry until well browned.

2. Add the crushed tomatoes, basil, salt, sugar, and pepper to the meat in the pan. Then add the kale and potatoes. Mix well. Reduce the heat and simmer 1½ hours, or until the potatoes are done.

VARIATION: Instead of the crushed tomatoes, basil, sugar, and pepper, pour Famous Tomato Sauce (see p. 69) into the pan along with the meat, kale, and potatoes.

¼ cup oil

6 garlic cloves, peeled and crushed

6 fresh pork hocks or pigs' feet (or a combination)

4 pounds 6 ounces (2 large cans) crushed tomatoes, with juice

2 teaspoons dried basil

2 teaspoons salt

2 teaspoons sugar

2 teaspoons coarsely ground black pepper

1 bunch fresh kale, washed and dried and cut in thirds

4 medium potatoes, peeled and cut in half

SUMMER SQUASH AND RED PEPPER SOUP

Serves 4–6

Not every summer soup needs to be served cold. Taste this light, yet filling, vegetable soup and you'll know why to make an exception.

1. In a food processor fitted with the steel blade, process the yellow squash until coarsely chopped. Set aside. Process the red pepper until coarsely chopped. Set aside. Process the onion until coarsely chopped.

2. Melt the butter in a skillet. Add the squash, red peppers, and onions and sauté over medium high heat for 10 minutes, or until well done.

3. Add the flour and mix well until the flour is absorbed. Continue to sauté for 5 more minutes.

4. Gradually pour in the chicken stock, stirring well, and simmer for 10 additional minutes.

5. Whisking continuously to avoid lumps, pour in the cream and add the salt and pepper. Heat the soup until it is hot but not boiling, and serve.

1 pound yellow squash, peeled, seeded, and cut in chunks

1 large red bell pepper, cored and seeded

1 medium onion, peeled and quartered

1 cup (2 sticks) butter

1/4 cup white flour

1 quart chicken stock

1/2 pint heavy cream

Salt and pepper to taste

ZUCCHINI SOUP WITH BASIL-PARMESAN BUTTER

Serves 4–6

Basil-parmesan butter can provide a surprise accent for more than this tasty soup. Try it as the finishing touch on vegetable dishes or beef stews.

In a mixing bowl, cream the butter and the basil, using a few drops of water to moisten the mixture. Add the salt and the Parmesan. Use immediately or freeze.

BASIL-PARMESAN BUTTER

2 tablespoons (1/4 stick) butter, at room temperature

1 tablespoon fresh basil, finely chopped

3 shakes salt

1/2 cup coarsely grated Parmesan cheese

1. Melt the butter in a 5-quart soup pot over medium high heat. Add the julienned zucchini and the chopped onions, along with the salt, pepper, basil, and bouillon cubes. Sauté the vegetables for 10 minutes.

2. Pour in the water and bring to a boil. Let the soup simmer, uncovered, for 1 hour.

3. To serve, ladle the soup into bowls and top with a dollop (or a chunk, if frozen) of the basil butter.

ZUCCHINI SOUP

4 tablespoons (1/2 stick) butter

5 medium zucchini, unpeeled and sliced julienne style

1 1/2 medium onions, peeled and chopped

1/2 teaspoon salt

1/2 teaspoon coarsely ground black pepper

1 tablespoon dried basil

6 chicken bouillon cubes, crushed

5 cups water

CREAM OF SPINACH SOUP

Serves 4–6

When was the last time you, not to mention your children, consumed a bag of spinach in less than ten minutes? When you make this fabulous soup, you'll be amazed at how quickly this creamy version of the nutritious vegetable disappears.

1. Melt 2 tablespoons of the butter in a shallow 4-quart pot or a Dutch oven. Add the onions and sauté over medium high heat. When the onions begin to brown, add the other 2 tablespoons of butter and all of the spinach.

2. Cook down the spinach until the leaves are totally wilted.

3. Pour in the chicken broth, bring to a boil, and let simmer for 5 minutes.

4. Remove the soup from the heat and purée in a food processor or a blender. (Be careful—the soup is hot. You can allow it to cool first, if you'd like.)

5. Return the soup to the pot. Add the cream, nutmeg, and the cheese if you're including it. Stir. Heat the soup until it is very hot but not boiling, and serve.

4 tablespoons (1/2 stick) butter

2 medium onions, peeled and sliced

20 ounces (2 bags) fresh spinach including leaves and stems, washed

6 cups chicken broth, canned or homemade

2 cups heavy cream

1 teaspoon nutmeg

2 cups grated Cheddar cheese or any one of your favorite cheeses (optional)

CREAM OF BROCCOLI SOUP

Serves 4–6

Use this soup to soothe away a chill.

1. Place the broccoli in a large pot and cover with water. Boil the broccoli 10 minutes, until still slightly firm. Drain and set aside.

2. Make a roux by melting half of the butter in a large saucepan or soup pot over medium high heat. Whisk in the flour. Continue to whisk the roux until it looks smooth. This should take about 2 minutes.

3. Gradually pour in the chicken broth, whisking constantly so that no lumps form. Remove from heat.

4. In a skillet, melt the other half of the butter over medium high heat. Sauté the boiled broccoli, along with the onion, in the skillet until both are tender.

5. Add the sautéed vegetables to the broth. Simmer, uncovered, for 15 to 20 minutes, stirring on occasion.

6. Purée the soup in batches in a blender or a food processor fitted with the steel blade until it is very smooth. Transfer the puréed soup to another pot.

7. Whisk in the cream. Heat the soup until it is hot, not boiling, and serve.

1 bunch broccoli, cut in chunks
8 tablespoons (1 stick) butter
1/3 cup flour
2 quarts chicken broth, canned or homemade
1 cup chopped onions
1 pint heavy cream

GRANDMA'S CHRISTMAS SOUP WITH LITTLE MEAT BALLS

Serves 4–6 as a main course; 8–10 as a first course

For my grandmother, there was no difference between a soup and a stock. Both began humbly, like this recipe, with bones or a chicken she had killed and cleaned herself. Both were also nourishing enough to feed her family and often, like her Christmas Soup, special enough to serve on the most important holidays.

1. Place the chicken in a very large soup pot (at least a 7-quart) capacity. Pour in the water. Add the celery, carrots, onion, salt, and pepper. Cook the soup on a low boil for 1½ hours. Meanwhile, prepare the chickory and the tiny meatballs.

SOUP
1 whole or cut-up chicken, 2½–3 pounds
6 quarts water

2. Cut both bunches of chickory in half. In a covered pot, boil the cut chickory until tender, about 20 minutes.

3. Strain the chickory well and then squeeze out any remaining water. Coarsely chop the chickory, and set aside while you make the meat balls.

1. In a large bowl, combine all of the ingredients except the oil. Mix thoroughly.

2. Between your hands, roll out approximately 65 tiny meat balls, each 1/2 to 3/4 of an inch in diameter, or about the size of a small walnut.

3. Heat the oil in a skillet over medium high heat and fry the meat balls, turning them as they cook, until all sides are browned. Drain the meat balls on a paper towel and set aside.

TO SERVE

1. Place the chopped chickory in a soup tureen. Using a slotted spoon, transfer the tiny meat balls to the tureen. Ladle the chicken stock over the chickory and meatballs.

2. Bone the chicken breast, dice into 1-inch pieces, and add to the soup. If you'd like, serve the remainder of the chicken with the vegetables on the side. Sprinkle generously with grated Romano cheese.

VARIATION: In a separate bowl, beat the eggs well in a little of the broth. Continuing to beat the eggs, as you pour them into the soup in a steady stream. They will form lovely yellow ribbons in the soup.

5 *celery ribs, including leaves, washed and cut in thirds*

2 *carrots, scraped and cut in half*

1 *large onion, peeled and left whole or quartered*

2 *tablespoons salt*

1/2 *teaspoon coarsely ground black pepper*

2 *bunches chickory*
  Coarsely grated Romano cheese

4 *eggs (optional)*

TINY MEAT BALLS

1 *pound lean ground beef*

1 *cup coarsely grated Romano cheese*

2 *eggs, slightly beaten*

3 *tablespoons coarsely chopped Italian parsley*

1/2 *cup bread crumbs*

1/2 *cup oil*

BEEF SOUP WITH TORTELLINI

Serves 4–6

This is soup the way my grandmother used to make it. Practical as well as nourishing, it keeps well overnight or in the freezer. Its hearty flavors are even richer when the broth is given a second chance to simmer. Serve it as a main course with fresh bread and a salad. Enjoy the boiled beef with a little Parsley Sauce (see p. 74) on the side.

1. Place the soupbone or beef in a large (5-quart) soup pot. Pour in the 4 quarts of water. Add the carrots, celery, onion, parsley, pepper, and salt. Boil rapidly over high heat for 5 minutes.

2. Reduce heat to a low boil. Add the tomato paste and cook the soup, uncovered so that it will concentrate, for 1 hour.

3. In a separate pot, cook the tortellini until al dente. Rinse in cold water, then drain well and set aside.

4. Scoop ¾ cup tortellini into each bowl. Ladle in the broth of the soup. Top with a slice of toast sprinkled with Parmesan, if you'd like, and serve immediately, while it's steaming. Serve the vegetables on the side in a separate bowl.

1 large beef shinbone with meat or ½ pound lean stew beef, cut in 1-inch pieces

4 quarts (16 cups) water

3 carrots, scrubbed but not peeled

5 center ribs celery, with leaves

1 large onion, peeled and quartered

2 heaping tablespoons coarsely chopped Italian parsley

1 heaping teaspoon coarsely ground black pepper

2 tablespoons salt

6 ounces (1 can) tomato paste

1 pound meat tortellini

4–6 slices white bread, toasted (optional)

Coarsely grated Parmesan cheese (optional)

TENDERLOIN OF BEEF STEW WITH DUMPLINGS

I can complete this rich and savory stew in half the time it used to take my mother to cook it. The difference is that I can afford a better cut of meat now than she could then, and splurging on tenderloin makes this satisfying stew, which was always easy to prepare, a fast dish too. But you can always follow the same recipe using a less expensive cut. Just boil the beef twice as long.

1. In a Dutch oven, heat the oil over medium high heat. Add the beef, carrots, celery, onions, garlic, rosemary, pepper, and 1 teaspoon of the salt. Raise the heat to high and sauté together, stirring often. Sprinkle the flour over all and continue to brown the meat and cook the vegetables until all of the liquid has evaporated.

2. Pour in the wine. Boil, stirring, for 3 minutes. Add the water and potatoes along with the other teaspoon of salt. Let the stew return to a boil.

3. Reduce the heat again to medium high and boil the stew fast for 30 minutes. Then prepare the dumplings.

VARIATION: For a sweeter stew, use 1 cup port instead of Burgundy.

STEW

- 1/3 cup olive oil
- 2 pounds beef tenderloin, cut in 1-inch pieces
- 1 1/2 cups carrots, cut in 1/2-inch rounds
- 1 celery stalk (without leaves), cut in 1/4-inch pieces
- 1 medium onion, peeled and sliced
- 3 garlic cloves, peeled and minced
- 1/4 teaspoon dried rosemary
- 1 teaspoon coarsely ground black pepper
- 2 teaspoons salt
- 2 tablespoons flour
- 1 cup Burgundy wine (or see VARIATION)
- 6 cups water
- 6 new red potatoes, peeled and cut in half

1. Combine the flour, baking powder, and salt in a bowl and mix well. With a fork, blend in the shortening. Pour in the milk and mix together to form a thick paste.

2. Drop the paste by tablespoonfuls on top of the boiling stew. Cook the dumplings with the stew, uncovered, for 10 minutes. Then cover the Dutch oven and cook for 10 more minutes.

DUMPLINGS

- 1 1/2 cups flour
- 2 teaspoons baking powder
- 1/2 teaspoon salt
- 1 tablespoon shortening
- 3/4 cup milk

ITALIAN FISH SOUP

Serves 4–6

As with its French cousin bouillabaisse, back in Italy the ingredients in fish soup vary according to the region, even the particular restaurant, and the day's catch. Our easily assembled version of this Mediterranean favorite is practical as well as delicious since the fish it calls for are readily available in New England. If monkfish and cod aren't available where you live, you can substitute other white-fleshed fish. It's a great dish to make for, and with, friends.

1. Heat the oil in a skillet over high heat. Add the fennel seed and brown until almost burned.

2. Reduce heat to medium. Add the fresh fennel and onions and sauté until translucent, about 10 minutes.

3. Add the tomatoes along with the monkfish, cod, and squid. Add the wine. Pour in the clam juice and stir. Bring the soup to a boil and simmer, uncovered, for another 20 minutes.

4. Reduce heat to low. Season with the saffron, pepper, and salt. Now simmer the soup for 1 hour.

5. Just before serving, sprinkle in the parsley. Serve steaming hot with crusty bread.

1/2 cup olive oil

1 tablespoon whole fennel seed

2 bulbs fresh fennel, sliced

2 large yellow onions, sliced

1 pound, 12 ounces (1 can) plum tomatoes, with juice

1 pound monkfish, cubed

1 pound cod, cubed

1/2 pound squid, cleaned and cut in rings

1/2 cup white wine

2 quarts clam juice

Pinch saffron

2 teaspoons coarsely ground black pepper

Salt to taste

1 bunch Italian parsley, finely chopped

ZUPPA DI TONNO

Italians are well-known for their tuna sauces, but tuna soup? I was apprehensive, to say the least, when Christina Dierker, a customer and friend, brought me a quart of tuna soup made by her grandmother, Margaret Pini. One look at the beautiful color, one whiff of the wonderful aroma, and then one spoonful of this soup and all my doubts disappeared.

1. Heat the oil in a large pot. Sauté the onions and garlic in the oil about 10 minutes, until translucent, but not yet brown.

2. Stir in the tomatoes, chicken broth, white beans, vermouth or sherry, salt, basil, oregano, and rosemary. Simmer, uncovered, for 15 minutes.

3. Stir in the sliced zucchini and simmer for 10 minutes more.

4. Stir in the tuna and continue to simmer until heated through.

5. Ladle the soup into individual serving bowls, sprinkle with the parsley, and serve with garlic bread or focaccia.

2 tablespoons olive oil

1 yellow onion, peeled and chopped

1 garlic clove, peeled and minced

1 pound canned tomatoes, peeled, seeded, and chopped, without juice

4 cups chicken broth or stock (preferably homemade)

1 pound canned cannelini beans

2 cups Vermouth or dry sherry

1 teaspoon salt

1 tablespoon fresh basil or 1 teaspoon dried basil

1 teaspoon dried oregano

1 teaspoon dried rosemary

2 large unpeeled zucchini, sliced in 1/8-inch pieces

13 ounces canned tuna, drained of oil or water

Fresh parsley for garnish

FISH AND SHELLFISH

LONG BEFORE ANYONE EVER TALKED ABOUT THE NUTRItional value of seafood, before scientists discovered we could help prevent heart disease with a regular dose of Omega 3, before our restaurants served sushi or salmon *en papillotte,* my grandfather, Louis Trio, provided fresh fish for his family. What's so unusual about that? you may well ask. Italians had been relying on their seas and inland lakes for food ever since Roman times. But my grandfather was a boss at a coke plant in Thompson, Pennsylvania. And there, in the middle of coal-mining country, finding fresh fish wasn't easy.

A native Sicilian, my grandfather missed the scampi and sardines he had eaten as a child; a shrewd businessman, he recognized an opportunity to turn this loss into his, and everyone's, gain. My aunt, Jenny Trio Grace, recalls that my grandfather found other families in town who were also interested in getting fresh fish. Then, when he had enough customers, my grandfather single-handedly made this previously unknown luxury available in Thompson. He got on the phone and placed orders for fresh fish with wholesalers in Boston.

Three times a year the fish and shellfish arrived. In those days before refrigeration, it was packed in ice, in big twenty-five-gallon barrels. My grandfather had a car but didn't drive, and so always asked someone to go behind the wheel so he could meet the incoming freight train carrying his orders. He loaded the barrels in the car, where he had more ice ready, then went home to distribute the fish and begin cooking himself.

There was eel inside some of the barrels, which my grandfather would mix in a white broth with garlic and oil. He fried the smelts he had bought as though they were fresh sardines, and he cooked the squid in spaghetti sauce. My grandfather taught his children how to grill the fresh shrimp that they grabbed from the barrels right in their shells, eating them when they turned pink. His own favorite was the oysters, so popular up and down the Atlantic coast, which my grandfather cooked in stew or, as they did back in Boston, ate raw on the half shell.

Without Louis Trio there never would have been any fresh fish or shellfish in Thompson or neighboring Republic, where I grew up. And when my grandfather died, shortly after I was born, the people once again learned to do without. Of course, we and the other Italian families in town somehow always managed to find the necessary ingredients for a traditional meatless Christmas Eve dinner. But this once-a-year meal, consisting of spaghetti with tuna sauce, eel in broth, fried smelts and shrimp, and baccalà stew, was all I ever experienced of fish until we moved to Cambridge. There my father took up where his father had left off, buying a boat to catch his own mackerel, cod, and flounder in Boston Harbor.

Since then, I, too, have learned to appreciate fresh fish and shellfish. When buying for my family or the store, I favor varieties native to our New England waters. I look for whole fish with clear eyes and firm flesh, and for fish and shellfish without too strong an odor. Back in my kitchen, whether frying, poaching, baking or whatever, I try never to overcook fish or overwhelm its delicate flavor. All of the recipes in this chapter can be prepared with frozen fish, but—as my grandfather showed—freshness is a thing of value and well worth any additional effort or expense. ◆

ITALIAN BAKED FISH

Serves 4

I love to spread a good topping over a firm-fleshed white fish. The preparation is easy, the presentation appealing, and the taste terrific.

1. Arrange the fish in an oiled baking dish. Set aside.

2. Melt the butter in a skillet over medium high heat. Add the chopped onions and garlic and sauté until the onions are browned.

3. Using your hands, crush the Ritz crackers into the skillet. Stir thoroughly, and remove skillet from heat.

4. Mix the Romano cheese, black pepper, and parsley into the crackers and onions to complete the topping.

5. Spread the topping over the fish. Pour the lemon juice over the topping. Bake the fish in a 400-degree oven for 40 minutes.

2 pounds fresh thick scrod, cod, haddock, or fillet of sole

Oil for baking dish

1/2 cup (1 stick) butter

1 medium onion, peeled and coarsely chopped

2 garlic cloves, peeled and coarsely chopped

36 (1 package) Ritz crackers

1 cup coarsely grated Romano cheese

1 tablespoon coarsely ground black pepper

1 cup coarsely chopped Italian parsley

Juice of 2 lemons

SCALLOPS IN BUTTER

Serves 4–6

Tiny, tender bay scallops prepared this way and mounded in scallop serving shells with lemon wedges make a delectable appetizer or light entrée with a salad.

1. Melt the butter in a skillet over medium high heat. Add the scallops and sauté for 5 minutes.

2. Meanwhile, crush the Ritz crackers by hand. Add the crushed crackers to the skillet to absorb the butter and cook, together with the scallops, for 3 minutes.

VARIATION: Sauté 2 finely minced garlic cloves in the butter for 3 minutes. Add the scallops, then the crackers. When the butter is absorbed, squeeze the juice of a fresh lemon over all, mix thoroughly, and serve.

1 cup (2 sticks) butter

1 pound bay scallops

54 Ritz crackers

BLUEFISH WITH NEW POTATOES

Serves 4–6

Bluefish shows its strength in the seas and in the kitchen. It thrives abundantly along the Italian coast as it does in our own East coast waters. And, paired with other strong flavors as in this recipe, the oily, robust blue will also thrive on your palate.

1. Slice the new potatoes about 1/4 inch thick.

2. In a roasting pan, combine the sliced potatoes with 1/2 cup of the olive oil, along with all the basil, garlic, salt, and pepper. Mix well. Bake the mixture in a 425-degree oven for 30 minutes. Remove potatoes from oven and reduce heat to 375 degrees.

3. Arrange the bluefish in another roasting pan or casserole dish, skin side down. Mound the roasted potatoes on top of the fish, leaving some of the fish's surface uncovered. Drizzle the remaining olive oil over the fish.

4. Bake the fish and the potatoes for 30 minutes, or until the potatoes become crispy.

1 1/2 pounds new potatoes, with skin

3/4 cup olive oil

1/2 cup chopped fresh basil, or 1 tablespoon dried

12 large garlic cloves, peeled and minced

Salt and pepper to taste

3 pounds (preferably fresh) whole bluefish fillet, with skin

BROILED SWORDFISH

Serves 4

Baking any fish can be a touchy affair, swordfish in particular. How can you tell when the meat is cooked through but not dried out? Some cooks measure any fish at its thickest point and cook it for 10 minutes per inch, according to the so-called Canadian rule, while others wait for the moment when there's no resistance to a press of the finger to say the fish is done. Personally, I'd rather not add to all this confusion, so I always broil swordfish.

1. Preheat the broiler.

2. Blend the oil, lemon juice, mint, oregano, salt, and pepper in a bowl. Using about a third of this blend, brush both sides of the swordfish.

3. Place the fish on the broiler rack about 4 inches below the flame. Broil for 7 minutes. Using another third of the lemon and oil blend, brush one side of the fish, turn it, and then brush the other side. Broil for 7 minutes more on this second side. Brush both sides of the fish one more time and serve.

1/4 cup olive oil

Juice of 2 lemons

1 tablespoon chopped fresh mint

3 teaspoons dried oregano

Salt and pepper to taste

2 pounds fresh swordfish steak, 1 1/2 inches thick

BALSAMIC SWORDFISH

Serves 10–12 as an appetizer; 4–6 for lunch

These days we usually think of any cold fish in a marinade as a South American specialty. But what could be more Italian than fish with peppers in balsamic vinegar, and what dish could be more perfect at a warm-weather lunch, light supper, or picnic?

1. Cut the swordfish into large cubes.

2. Heat the oil in a large skillet over high heat. Add the swordfish cubes and brown all sides well. Remove the fish from the skillet with a slotted spoon and reserve.

3. Using the same skillet, sauté the onions and peppers in the remaining oil until the onion slices are almost transparent and the peppers are wilted.

4. Reduce the heat to medium. Gently transfer the swordfish back to the skillet, along with any juices, taking care not to break the cubes. Pour in the vinegar. Season with the pepper and salt and cook together for 5 minutes.

5. Transfer the swordfish, vegetables, and sauce to a large bowl and chill for at least 2 hours. Serve cold on a bed of lettuce.

2 pounds fresh swordfish

1 cup olive oil

1 large yellow onion, peeled and sliced

1 red, 1 green, and 1 yellow bell pepper, each cored, seeded, and sliced lengthwise in thin strips

1½ cups balsamic vinegar

1 tablespoon coarsely ground black pepper

1 teaspoon salt

FRIED SMELTS, DAD'S STYLE

Serves 4–6

To replace his native Italian sardine, my grandfather, Louis Trio, started frying the leaner but similar-tasting smelt. My father continued his father's tradition once a year, preparing crispy smelts for our Christmas Eve dinner. Today I enjoy fried smelts any time, especially with boiled new potatoes and a salad. The center bone can be easily removed in one piece just before eating.

1. Pour the flour into a plastic bag. Drop 6 smelts into the bag and shake the bag to coat the fish. Repeat until you have coated all the smelts.

2. Heat the oil in an 8-inch skillet over medium high heat.

3. When the oil is hot, arrange the coated smelts in the skillet. Fry the fish for about 5 minutes, turning often until all sides are golden. (Be careful not to overcook—the smelts will fall apart.)

4. With a slotted spoon, remove the smelts from the skillet and place them on paper towels to drain. After sprinkling them with salt, serve the smelts at once on a beautiful platter.

1 cup flour
1 1/2 pounds fresh smelts (cleaned and with heads removed)
2 cups oil
Salt

BACCALÀ STEW

Serves 4–6

This is a slightly sweet stew that looks good and smells divine. It seems appropriate, with an aroma like this, that my grandmother made this family recipe only once a year, on Christmas Eve.

1. Place the pieces of baccalà in a 3-quart saucepan and rinse off the salt with cold water. Drain. Then, leaving the fish in, fill the pot with fresh cold water. Bring to a boil and immediately drain. Repeat this process twice. Then set the fish aside.

2. Pour the oil into a large pot with at least a 5-quart capacity. Fry the sliced onions in the oil over high heat until they are browned.

1 pound boneless salted cod (baccalà), cut in 3-inch pieces
1 1/2 cups oil
3 medium onions, peeled and sliced
12 ounces (2 cans) tomato paste
2 quarts (8 cups) water

3. Leaving the heat on high, stir in the tomato paste and let cook 1 minute. Pour in the water and stir well.

4. When the mixture returns to a boil, stir in the baccalà, chestnuts, raisins, and bay leaves. Add the pepper and sugar. Continue to cook on a low simmer, uncovered, for 2½ hours, stirring on occasion. Remove the bay leaves and serve.

2½ cups roasted chestnuts, or jarred chestnuts, not in syrup
1½ cups raisins
3 bay leaves
½ teaspoon coarsely ground black pepper
4 tablespoons sugar

SHRIMP WITH PINK PEPPERCORN SAUCE

Serves 4–6

The extra-smooth sauce is a subdued shade of pink; the sautéed shrimp seem to melt in your mouth. In every way, this dish is the height of good taste. Serve it on a bed of homemade pink peppercorn macaroni (see p. 31) when you really want to impress someone special.

1. Melt the butter in a large skillet over medium high heat. Place the shrimp in the skillet and sauté for 2 minutes.

2. Add the minced garlic, ginger, and ground pink peppercorns. Sauté together for 3 more minutes.

3. Using a slotted spoon, remove the shrimp from the skillet and reserve. Add the scallions to the remaining mixture and sauté for 2 minutes.

4. Pour the heavy cream into the skillet. Add any juice given off by the reserved shrimp. With the heat still on medium high, cook this sauce for 10 minutes or until its volume is reduced by about a third.

5. Reduce the heat to medium. Return the shrimp to the skillet. Cook all together for 2 additional minutes and serve.

8 tablespoons (1 stick) butter
2 pounds jumbo shrimp, shelled and deveined
1 tablespoon minced garlic
2 tablespoons freshly grated gingerroot
1 tablespoon pink peppercorns, ground in a food processor or crushed with a mallet
1 bunch scallions, chopped
1 pint heavy cream

STUFFED SQUID

It seems that almost every Southern Italian family has its own recipe for stuffed squid. This tasty, tomato-ey version of what is usually considered a holiday dish comes from my friend Gilda, whose mother used to cook squid in sauce like this in her small town outside Naples, and from Gilda's husband, Joe. The only secret here is to be sure to buy large squid whose cavities are so much easier to fill.

1. Place the squid in a saucepan and cover with water. Bring the water to a boil, reduce the heat, and simmer for 5 minutes. Remove saucepan from heat and drain the squid. Rinse with cold water and drain again. Reserve.

2. With your hands, squash the tomatoes into another saucepan. Pour in the tomato juice from the can. Add 2 tablespoons of the oil, half the garlic, 1 pinch salt, 1 pinch pepper, and 1 tablespoon of the parsley. Stir. Cook on low heat, covered, for 45 minutes to 1 hour until the sauce thickens.

4. Meanwhile, combine the other half of the minced garlic, 1 pinch salt, 1 pinch pepper, and the remaining tablespoon of parsley with the white of the bread, the eggs, cheese, and the other tablespoon of oil in a bowl. Using your hands, mix this stuffing well.

5. Pack the stuffing into the body of each squid. (Don't pack too tightly, and stop just before the top of each cavity.) Pin each stuffed squid closed with a toothpick or skewer.

6. When the sauce is cooked, add the stuffed squid to the saucepan. Cover and cook together for 10 to 12 minutes.

2 pounds large fresh squid without the tentacles, cleaned

1 pound (1 can) whole, peeled tomatoes, with juice

3 tablespoons oil

4 garlic cloves, peeled and minced

2 pinches salt

2 pinches coarsely ground black pepper

2 tablespoons coarsely chopped Italian parsley

4 cups (preferably day-old, otherwise fresh) coarsely chopped Italian bread (white part only)

3 eggs, beaten

1 tablespoon coarsely grated Romano cheese

Stuffed squid shouldn't be packed too tightly.

CALAMARI SALAD

Serves 6 as an appetizer; 4 as an entrée

Like many shellfish, calamari is equally good hot and cold. And this Calamari Salad (Scicche Insalata di Calamari in Italian) is a staple at Cremaldi's all summer long. The garlic and lemon combine to give it a tangy, tantalizing taste, and it looks wonderful served on lettuce or other greens. With just a loaf of bread you've got a whole summer meal.

1. Place calamari in a large saucepan and cover with water. When water comes to a boil, lower heat and simmer 15 minutes. Drain and chill by rinsing in cold water. Drain well.

2. Slice calamari bodies across in 1/4-inch rings, being careful to remove any cartilage that might have been left in. Leave tentacles whole if they are small; slice large ones in half. Place all the calamari in a large mixing bowl.

3. Add the rest of the ingredients and mix well with a spoon. Serve on a bed of lettuce and garnish with a lemon wedge.

3 pounds calamari, cleaned

1 small whole head of garlic, each clove peeled and minced

1 bunch fresh basil, washed and chopped

1/2 teaspoon crushed red pepper

Juice of 2 lemons

Peel of 1 lemon, finely minced

1/3 cup olive oil

1 cup red vinegared peppers (available in jars at many supermarkets and Italian specialty shops), slivered

1 tablespoon vinegar from peppers

1/2 teaspoon coarsely ground black pepper

1 teaspoon salt

MEATS AND POULTRY

B

Y THE TIME I WAS TWELVE YEARS OLD, I COULD CUT A fuller veal pocket, barbecue a juicier piece of pork, and pluck a chicken better than any other kid I knew. Knowing my circumstances, such expertise might seem surprising. It's true that acres of cornfields for grazing surrounded our house, but we never owned a cow. My grandfather had run a slaughterhouse back in Sicily, but a Republic, Pennsylvania, town ordinance outlawed the raising of pigs several years before I was born. My grandmother did on occasion break the necks of the chickens in her coop, despite our childish protests, but I refused to bear witness to the bloody deed. In fact, fresh meat of any kind was a rarity at our table, a luxury as costly as it was often unobtainable. So where, then, did I hone my butcher's skills, if not at home? Simply by going down the road and entering the plain wooden flat-topped building that was Cozy Nook, our family's hamburger joint.

It was supposed to have been my mother's sister Mary who ran Cozy's, mainly for the kids and teachers at Red Stone Township High School, just across the street. But when Mary's husband decided he wasn't too happy living in a small town, my grandmother purchased the place with its booths and jukebox and when she got tired my mother took over. Watching my mother cook in Cozy's kitchen, I confronted more veal breasts, pork shoulders, feathered birds, and raw chuck than I ever knew existed. Suddenly we had a ready supply of fresh meat and poultry, and with this newfound wealth, my previous notions of the food underwent a small revolution.

Whereas before I had eaten lean ground beef only with spaghetti, in my grandmother's soup, or flattened into a giant oval in my father's fancy meatball, now I could indulge in the best burgers in the world from our own grill any time. The only way I had known pork before Cozy's was roasted with garlic, but for her customers my mother sliced pork thin and barbecued it in a special blend of tomato, celery, and onion. My mother even took liberties with the most costly meat of all, batter-dipping chunks of veal and serving them, along with pork, on a taffy-apple stick for a dish we called "city chicken." And as for chicken itself, usually roasted in so stately a manner at home, it now appeared for popular consumption fried, Southern style.

To me, our kitchen at home and the one at Cozy Nook were worlds apart. The former represented a traditional approach to food, the latter the tastes of the younger generation. What I failed to see were their similarities—the bread crumbs rolled into my Dad's fancy meat ball and Cozy's burgers, for instance, or the pork and veal combination in a family cacciatore and "city chicken," or the egg batter used for that specialty on a stick and for veal parmigiana. Today I know that you can begin with the same cut of fresh meat, but if you slice it instead of chunk it or steam it instead of bake it or alter one step in the recipe, you end up with a dish that looks and tastes entirely different. Chicken really is the most versatile of foods, as many cooks claim, and veal the most neutral. That's why in this chapter there are meat and poultry recipes that come straight from my family's table, while others that start with many of the same ingredients end up more in the style of grown-up kids who like to sit in the booths. ◆

MY FATHER'S VEAL POCKET

Serves 4–6

This veal pocket must cook slowly. That's why my father would put it in the oven early on Sunday morning so that by the time we children woke up, hours later, the wonderful aroma was already wafting through the house. Sometimes my father would sharpen the filling with salami, or roast potatoes along with the veal. Like the best of our family dishes, this veal pocket was always improvised, open to spur-of-the-moment inspirations.

1. Heat the butter in a skillet over medium high heat. Sauté the mushrooms in the butter until soft, about 5 minutes.

2. For the filling, in a large bowl combine the ground beef, parsley, bread crumbs, 1 tablespoon of the black pepper, garlic powder, eggs, sliced olives, pine nuts, and the sautéed mushrooms. Mix well by hand.

3. Pack this filling into the veal pocket tightly. Place the stuffed veal in a baking pan. Pour the 2 cups of water

2 tablespoons (1/4 stick) butter

1/2 pound mushrooms, sliced

1 pound lean ground beef

1 cup coarsely chopped Italian parsley

1 cup plain bread crumbs

1 tablespoon plus 1 teaspoon coarsely ground black pepper

into the bottom of the pan. Place the garlic cloves and the bay leaves in the water. Sprinkle the veal with the teaspoon of black pepper, along with the rosemary and salt.

4. Cover the pan tightly with aluminum foil and bake in a 400-degree oven for 45 minutes.

5. Uncover the veal. Lower the oven temperature to 325 degrees. Continue to cook the veal for an additional 1½ hours, basting every 15 minutes and adding more water if necessary. You can add potatoes around the veal pocket about 1 hour before it is done. To serve, slice the veal pocket lengthwise and spoon on the pan juices.

NOTE: To cut a veal pocket, use a sharp knife. Make short cuts with the knife, lifting the meat away from the bone as you slice. Cut as close to the rib as you can, making a pocket and leaving about 1 inch all around the edge of the veal breast.

1 teaspoon garlic powder

3 eggs, beaten

20 oil-cured pitted black olives, sliced in quarters

3 tablespoons pine nuts

3 pound veal breast (ask butcher to make pocket or cut your own—see NOTE below)

2 cups water

4 garlic cloves, unpeeled and left whole

2 bay leaves

1 tablespoon dried rosemary leaves

1 teaspoon salt

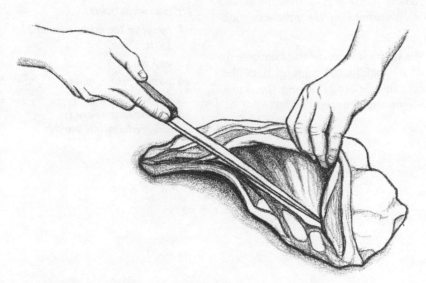

Use one hand to lift the top half of the veal pocket away from the bone as you cut through the meat.

VEAL PEZZITINE

Pezzitine means chunks or little pieces. And when my friend and neighbor Lena Pissinis Waldron was a child living on a farm in Italy during the Second World War, little pieces, once a month, was all the veal she got. Today this once rationed meal has become a regular feature at Lena's family table. She likes to serve the succulent chunks of veal in wine sauce with mashed potatoes on the side.

1. Melt the butter and oil in a large skillet over medium heat. Add the chopped garlic and sauté until browned, about 5 minutes.

2. Add the veal to the browned garlic in the skillet. Sprinkle in the salt and pepper and raise the heat to medium high. Cover and cook, stirring frequently, for 10 to 15 minutes until the butter and oil have almost disappeared.

3. Pour the wine into the skillet. Dissolve the tomato paste in the water and pour this into the skillet too ("to give the sauce a little color," Lena says). Cover the skillet and, with the heat still on medium high, continue to cook for 5 more minutes.

4. Add the peas. Stir the veal mixture and continue to cook, covered, for 5 to 10 additional minutes until the veal is nice and tender. Just before removing the skillet from the heat, sprinkle on the chopped parsley.

4 tablespoons (1/2 stick) butter

3 tablespoons oil

5 garlic cloves, peeled and chopped

1 1/2 pounds veal fillet or stew meat, cut into 1 1/2 inch cubes

1 teaspoon salt

1 teaspoon coarsely ground black pepper

1/2 cup white wine

1 heaping teaspoon tomato paste

1/2 cup water

10 ounces frozen peas, loosened

3 tablespoons coarsely chopped Italian parsley

VEAL AND SAUSAGE CACCIATORE

Italians consume more veal than anyone else and seem never to run out of ways to serve it. Pairing veal with sausages in this hunter-style dish is yet another great flavor combination.

1. Cut the veal into bite-sized pieces. Slice each sausage link into thirds.

2. Heat the oil in a deep skillet over medium high heat. Meanwhile, dredge the veal in the flour and place the pieces in the hot oil.

3. Add the minced garlic and the black pepper to the skillet and fry the veal, turning often. After about 5 minutes, when the veal is browned, add the sausage. Fry together for another 5 minutes.

4. Add the mushrooms, the green and red pepper strips, and the additional 1/4 cup oil, if the meats are sticking to the skillet. Cook for about 10 more minutes, until the peppers start to wilt, stirring fairly often.

5. Stir in the tomatoes, along with the salt and sugar. Reduce the heat to low. Simmer, uncovered, for about 30 minutes, until the peppers are cooked through, stirring occasionally. This is a good dish to serve over homemade macaroni.

1 pound veal fillet

4 links hot Italian fennel sausage (see p. 145)

1/2 cup oil plus 1/4 cup (if necessary)

Flour for dredging

3 large garlic cloves, peeled and minced

1 heaping teaspoon coarsely ground black pepper

1 green and 1 red bell pepper, or 2 green peppers, cored, seeded and sliced in narrow strips

1 pound mushrooms, sliced in 1/4–1/2-inch pieces

2 pounds (2 cans) crushed peeled tomatoes, with juice

1/2 teaspoon salt

1/2 teaspoon sugar

VEAL FILLETS IN LEMON AND CAPER SAUCE

Serves 4

When I first started selling veal in a plain lemon sauce, I never realized something was missing. But customers kept asking why I didn't include capers, as though it were the most natural and necessary of ingredients. As soon as I added the piquant buds of the caper bush I understood what they meant. Now I wonder how I ever made this rich dish without them.

1. Melt the butter and oil in a 10-inch skillet over medium high heat. Meanwhile dredge the veal in the flour and place it in the heated skillet.

2. Quickly fry the veal for about 2 or 3 minutes on each side, so that both sides of each fillet are slightly browned. Transfer the veal to your serving platter and reserve.

3. Add the lemon juice and the capers to the same skillet and let simmer for just 30 seconds. Pour in the beef broth and simmer for 3 minutes more. Remove the skillet from heat, then add the parsley. Stir well.

4. Spoon the capers and parsley mixture over the fillets and serve, garnished with thin lemon slices.

12 tablespoons (1½ sticks) butter

¼ cup oil

6 veal fillets, about 4 ounces each

1 cup flour for dredging

Juice of 1 lemon

1 cup capers in brine, drained

1 cup beef broth

1 bunch Italian parsley, coarsely chopped

Lemon slices for garnish

VEAL ROLL IN MUSTARD CREAM

Serves 10–12

Your guests will look at the elegant presentation of this dish and think you've spared no expense. The pan juices provide the base for the sauce, and as Laura Ridge, the professional cook who created the dish for Cremaldi's, conveniently discovered, frozen spinach works as well as the fresh vegetable here. Serve the veal slices on a bed of homemade fettucine and your meal is complete.

1. Melt the butter in a skillet over high heat. Sauté the chopped onion for about 4 minutes, until the pieces become transparent. Add the garlic to the skillet and sauté with the onions for another minute or so.

2. Stir in the spinach and pine nuts. Continue to stir as you pour in one cup of the wine, mix in the Romano, and

VEAL ROLL

8 tablespoons (1 stick) butter

1 large onion, peeled and chopped

4 garlic cloves, peeled and minced

season with the white pepper. Remove the stuffing from the heat.

3. Open up the veal leg. Spoon the stuffing generously on top of the veal. Spread evenly, leaving a 1-inch margin along the perimeter of the leg.

4. Roll the veal. Slip the strings underneath the rolled veal and tie them separately at equal intervals along the veal roll.

5. Set the veal roll on a rack in a shallow roasting pan. Sprinkle the veal with the black pepper and drizzle with the olive oil. Pour the other cup of white wine into the bottom of the pan.

6. Cook the veal roll in a 400-degree oven for 2 hours, or until your meat thermometer reads 140–150 degrees. Baste with pan juices on occasion. Remove the veal from the oven and let it stand for 30 minutes. Meanwhile, make the sauce.

1. Strain the pan juices.

2. Melt the butter in a heavy-bottomed saucepan over medium high heat. Stir in the flour to create a roux. Cook for 2 to 3 minutes, stirring continuously to make sure the roux does not turn brown.

3. Reduce the heat to medium. Whisk in the pan juices and the stock. Stir in the mustard and the heavy cream. The consistency of the sauce will become like a thick gravy that coats the spoon.

4. Season the sauce with the tarragon, white pepper, and salt to taste. Reduce the heat to low and stir the sauce occasionally as you cook it, uncovered, for 10 more minutes.

5. Cut the strings on the veal roll and remove. Slice the veal as thin as possible.

6. Put a spoonful of the sauce onto each guest's plate and arrange a slice of the veal on top. Serve immediately. Pass extra sauce in a gravy boat.

2 *packages frozen spinach, thawed and drained,* or 2 *pounds fresh spinach, washed and chopped*

1/2 *cup pine nuts*

2 *cups dry white wine*

1 *cup coarsely grated Romano cheese*

1 *teaspoon white pepper*

5 *pounds boneless leg of veal*

4 *18-inch pieces butcher's twine (ask butcher to wrap twine separately)*

1 *teaspoon coarsely ground black pepper*

3 *tablespoons olive oil*

SAUCE

All of the pan juices

1/2 *cup (1 stick) butter*

1/2 *cup flour*

2 *cups veal or chicken stock (preferably homemade)*

3/4 *cup Dijon-style prepared mustard*

1 *cup heavy cream*

2 *tablespoons chopped fresh tarragon,* or 1 *teaspoon dry*

1/2 *teaspoon white pepper*

Salt, to taste

VEAL CUTLETS PARMIGIANA

So good, you'll think you're eating this great dish for the very first time.

1. In a shallow dish, combine the Romano, bread crumbs, minced garlic, parsley, and 1 teaspoon of the black pepper. Set aside.

2. In another shallow dish, beat the eggs with the 2 tablespoons of water.

3. Dip the pieces of veal into the beaten eggs, then into the cheese and bread crumb mixture, coating both sides.

4. Meanwhile, heat the oil in a large skillet over medium high heat. Place the breaded veal in the skillet and fry until golden brown, about 3 minutes on each side. Remove the cutlets and arrange in a shallow pan or baking dish.

5. In the same skillet, combine the tomatoes, the cup of water, salt, 1/2 teaspoon of pepper, basil, and sugar. Mix well and boil fairly rapidly, uncovered, over medium high heat for 15 minutes to incorporate the flavors and thicken.

6. Ladle half of the sauce over the veal. Then place one slice of cheese over each cutlet. Add the remaining sauce and sprinkle the veal with the Parmesan.

7. Bake the veal parmigiana in a 400-degree oven for 20 minutes, or until the mozzarella is melted.

1 cup coarsely grated Romano cheese

1/2 cup plain bread crumbs

2 garlic cloves, peeled and minced

4 tablespoons finely chopped Italian parsley

1 1/2 teaspoons coarsely ground black pepper

2 eggs

2 tablespoons plus 1 cup water

6 veal fillets or cutlets, 4 ounces each

1 cup oil

1 pound, 12 ounces (1 can) crushed peeled tomatoes, with juice

1/2 teaspoon salt

1/2 teaspoon dried basil

1/2 teaspoon sugar

6 slices mozzarella cheese, 1/4 inch thick

3 tablespoons coarsely grated Parmesan cheese

BEEF BRACIOLA

This southern Italian specialty has long been popular here, probably because the rolled beef has three virtues not always found in a meat dish. Braciola offers variety in its fillings, an unusual presentation, and economy—a little of this steak goes a long way.

1. Holding your hand on top of the round steak, slice through it horizontally with a sharp knife to open the meat and double its size. (If you prefer, you can ask the butcher to cut a beef round thinly for braciola and skip this step.)

2. In a bowl, combine the bread crumbs, Romano cheese, garlic, parsley, and pepper. Mix well and sprinkle these stuffing ingredients over the whole opened piece of meat.

3. Slice the cooled hard-boiled eggs and place them on top of the stuffing. Then roll up the meat in jelly-roll fashion and tie it with the string in various places to hold it together.

4. Pour enough oil into a skillet to cover the bottom. Heat the oil and fry the rolled beef, turning often, until brown.

5. Transfer the beef to a baking pan. Pour the cup of water into the bottom of the pan. If you'd like potatoes, place them around the meat and sprinkle them with salt and coarsely ground black pepper.

6. Bake the braciola in a 375-degree oven for 1 hour, or until the potatoes are done, adding more water to the pan if necessary. Then remove the string, cut the meat into 1-inch slices, and serve.

VARIATION: Brown the rolled beef in a Dutch oven instead of a skillet. Then remove the meat from the Dutch oven. Combine 1 large can whole peeled tomatoes (with juice), 2 small cans tomato paste, 1 quart of water, and salt and pepper to taste in the Dutch oven and mix well. Return the meat to the Dutch oven and simmer over low heat for 1½ hours. Slice and serve with spaghetti instead of potatoes.

3-pound slice of round steak, 1½ inches thick

½ cups plain bread crumbs

1 cup coarsely grated Romano cheese

3 garlic cloves, peeled and finely minced

½ cup finely chopped Italian parsley

1 teaspoon coarsely ground black pepper, plus a sprinkling for potatoes

4 hard-boiled eggs, cooled

Kitchen string for trussing

Oil

1 cup water

Potatoes (optional)

Salt for sprinkling potatoes

TONY TRIO'S FANCY MEAT BALL

Serves 4–6

When I made this dish at the store, Rosie, our Italian cook, said with a look of recognition, "Oh, polpettone facito con le uova." (Translation: "A meat ball with eggs inside.") Apparently Italians have long enjoyed what we in my family always thought of as my father's novel approach to meat loaf. I understand why. It's a simple project with impressive and beautiful results.

1. Hard-boil 4 eggs. Peel and set aside.

2. Place the lean ground beef in a large mixing bowl. Put the garlic cloves through a garlic press and add to the meat along with the four uncooked eggs, Romano cheese, bread crumbs, parsley, and pepper. Combine all the ingredients thoroughly by hand. This meat mixture should be moist enough to pack down easily.

3. Flatten out the meat mixture to an oval approximately 12 × 8 inches and 1½ to 2 inches thick. Line the hard-boiled eggs across the middle of the oval lengthwise. Fold the meat over the eggs, creating a long oblong shape that looks like a roast.

4. Pour oil to a depth of 1/2 inch across the bottom of a Dutch oven or another pan large enough to fit the meat ball and sauce. Heat the oil on low heat. When the oil is very hot, place the meat ball in the pan and fry, turning as each side is browned. Transfer the meat ball to a plate. Then, in the same Dutch oven or pan, make the sauce.

MEAT BALL

- *8 eggs*
- *3 pounds lean ground beef*
- *3 garlic cloves, peeled*
- *1½ cups coarsely grated Romano cheese*
- *3/4 cups plain bread crumbs*
- *1/4 cup chopped Italian parsley*
- *1 heaping teaspoon coarsely ground black pepper*
- *Oil for frying*

1. Remove all but about a cup of the oil from the Dutch oven or pan where you cooked the meat ball. Leave any remaining chunks of cooked meat in the Dutch oven or pan too.

2. Using a garlic press, add the garlic to the oil and sauté for 3 minutes. Then add all the rest of the ingredients. Cook, uncovered, over medium heat for 30 minutes.

3. Reduce the heat and return the meat ball to the Dutch oven or pan. Let the meat ball simmer in the sauce for 1½ hours.

4. Gently transfer the meat ball to a large platter and let it stand 10 minutes. Slice the meat ball into rounds ½ inch thick. Arrange the slices either in a row or a circle on the platter and pour some sauce over the top of the slices. Pour the rest of the sauce over any shape macaroni you'd like and serve along with the meat ball.

SAUCE

Oil (already in Dutch oven or pan—see above)

2 garlic cloves, peeled

3½ pounds (2 large cans) ground, peeled tomatoes, with juice

3 tomato cans water

12 ounces (2 cans) tomato paste

1 tomato paste can water

1 teaspoon coarsely ground black pepper

2 teaspoons salt

1 heaping tablespoon dried basil, or 8 fresh basil leaves, chopped

1 tablespoon sugar

Serve your fancy meat ball on a bed of lettuce or spinach.

KIKI'S CHICKEN

This is the incomparable dish my cousin Kiki's father made one day when he walked out on his second wife carrying just his spices. He ended up in Kiki's kitchen where, working with only ingredients he had right there, he made this chicken. In this same spirit of spontaneity, this is one recipe where it's more fun to chop and dice as you go along, rather than do everything ahead of time. Be sure to really mound the cut vegetables on top of the bird so that you can hardly tell that there's a chicken underneath.

1. Place the chicken in a small roasting pan. Place one garlic clove inside each crease of the chicken legs.

2. Chop the celery into 2-inch pieces and quarter the onion. Stuff the quartered onion and celery inside the chicken cavity.

3. Sprinkle 1 teaspoon of the pepper, 1 teaspoon of the salt and all of the rosemary over the chicken.

4. Coarsely chop the parsley. Mound and pack the parsley over the chicken, together with the chopped basil. Dice the tomatoes in 1/2-inch pieces and mound them on top of the chicken too.

5. Sprinkle the other teaspoon of pepper and the other teaspoon of salt over the chicken. Put 6 dollops of shortening, a tablespoon each, over the surface of the chicken, on top of the vegetables.

6. Cover the roasting pan tightly with its cover or with aluminum foil. Bake the chicken in a 400-degree oven for 1 hour.

7. After an hour, uncover the chicken and pour the red wine over it. Continue to cook the chicken, uncovered, for another hour, basting every 15 minutes. Serve the chicken with all the cooked vegetables as a side dish and pan drippings as gravy.

VARIATION: You can make this recipe with turkey or even a beef roast.

5-pound roasting chicken, or 2 smaller (2–2 1/2-pound) roasting chickens

2 garlic cloves, peeled and left whole

1/2 bunch celery, with leaves

1 large yellow onion, peeled

2 teaspoons coarsely ground black pepper

2 teaspoons salt

1 heaping tablespoon dried rosemary leaves

1 bunch Italian parsley

2 cups chopped fresh basil

6 large tomatoes

6 tablespoons shortening

1 1/2 cups red wine

GRANDMA'S STEAMED CHICKEN AND POTATOES

There are two good versions of this nourishing meal in a dish. Simply steamed in water is how my grandmother used to cook the chicken back in Pennsylvania. Spruced up in my Ginger-Vermouth Sauce seems to be the way people with more sophisticated palates prefer this steamed chicken today.

1. Heat the oil in a 5-quart pot or Dutch oven over medium high heat. Add the chicken pieces and rosemary. Fry the chicken until brown.

2. Pour in the water or the Ginger-Vermouth Sauce. Add the potatoes and carrots, salt and pepper, and fresh string beans if you're using them. Cover the pot tightly with a lid. Reduce the heat and steam the chicken and vegetables together for about 1 hour, until the vegetables are tender.

3. If you're using frozen string beans, add them a few minutes before the chicken is done.

1 cup oil
   2 1/2–3-pound chicken, cut up
2 tablespoons dried rosemary leaves
1 cup water or 1 cup Ginger-Vermouth Sauce (see p. 00)
3 large potatoes, peeled and quartered
5 carrots, scraped and cut in 2-inch chunks
1 teaspoon salt
1 teaspoon coarsely ground black pepper
1 package (10 ounces) frozen whole string beans, thawed (optional), or 8 ounces fresh string beans, trimmed and washed

STUFFED CHICKEN BREASTS CAPOCOLLO

I love to combine capocollo and mozzarella on a sandwich. Tightly wrapped inside chicken breasts, the package presented with a simple sauce, this meat and cheese combination looks, and tastes, even better here.

1. Lay each chicken breast, skin side up, between sheets of wax paper. Pound each breast until it is flattened to 1/4 inch in thickness. Remove the wax paper.

2. Lay each breast skin side down. Arrange a third of the capocollo slices and a third of the mozzarella slices across the center of each breast.

3. Roll each chicken breast tightly. Place the stuffed, rolled chicken pieces in a 9 × 9-inch baking pan. (The three breasts should barely touch, just enough to support one another.)

4. Pour the stock over the chicken. Cover the pan with foil and bake in a 375-degree oven for 40 minutes. (During this time, prepare the sauce.) At the end of 40 minutes, uncover the pan and broil the chicken until browned.

1. In a Dutch oven, sauté the onions in the oil over medium high heat until they become translucent.

2. Add the mushrooms and sauté until tender, about 5 minutes.

3. Continuing to sauté, pour in the Madeira and the stock. Stir and let the sauce simmer for about 20 minutes, until the volume is reduced by half.

4. To serve, slice the chicken breasts. Spoon a puddle of the sauce onto each guest's plate and arrange a slice of chicken on top. Pass extra sauce in a gravy boat.

CHICKEN

3 whole boneless chicken breasts, with skin

1/2 pound capocollo, sliced 1/4 inch thick

1/4 pound mozzarella cheese, sliced 1/4 inch thick

1/2 cup chicken stock (homemade or canned)

SAUCE

3 tablespoons oil

1 medium yellow onion, peeled and diced

2 cups sliced mushrooms

1/2 cup Madeira or port

1 cup chicken stock (homemade or canned)

Salt and pepper to taste

STUFFED CHICKEN BREASTS VERMOUTH

Sometimes inventing a new recipe is as easy as pairing flavors that appeal to you. A Chappaqua, New York, friend would always bring me stuffed chicken breasts from her butcher when she came to visit. What better way to bake them, I thought, than with a topping soaked in one of my favorite liquors, vermouth?

1. Lay each chicken breast, skin side up, between sheets of wax paper. Pound each breast until it is flattened and spread a couple of inches larger.

2. Lay each breast skin side down. Sprinkle with 1/2 teaspoon of the pepper. Spread a teaspoon of butter over each breast. Then arrange a slice of Swiss cheese and a slice of ham across the center of each chicken piece.

3. Roll up each chicken breast. Using plain white string or sewing thread, tie each breast in two places, or as many places as you'd like, to hold it together.

4. Heat the oil in a skillet over medium high heat. Place the rolled chicken in the hot oil and brown until all sides are golden. Then transfer the breasts to a baking dish.

5. Using the same skillet, and with the heat still on medium high, melt the remaining butter. Add the mushrooms and onions and sauté together until the mushrooms are tender and the onions are just beginning to turn golden.

6. Continuing to sauté, stir in the vermouth and then the chicken broth. Remove the skillet from the heat.

7. Mound the sautéed mushroom and onion mixture on top of the rolled chicken breasts. Bake together, uncovered, in a 400-degree oven for 45 minutes. Serve topped with the mushroom and onion mixture.

4 **whole boneless chicken breasts, with skin**

2 **teaspoons coarsely ground black pepper**

3/4 **cup (1 1/2 sticks) butter, at room temperature**

4 **slices Swiss cheese**

4 **slices boiled Danish ham**

1/2 **cup oil**

1 **pound mushrooms (if large, slice in 1/4-inch chunks; if small, halve)**

2 **large onions, peeled and sliced**

1/2 **cup vermouth**

1/2 **cup chicken broth (homemade or canned)**

CHICKEN BREASTS WITH PEPPERONI MOUSSE

Serves 4–6

With its array of bright colors mixed like handfuls of confetti, the unusual filling to this chicken will give you cause to cheer. But you don't need a ticker-tape parade to serve this delightful dish, just a reason to turn a simple occasion into a special celebration.

1. Lay each of the five chicken breasts, skin side up, between sheets of wax paper. Hammer each breast until it is flattened and spread a couple of inches larger. (Try to make each piece the same size.) Set aside.

2. Remove outer casing and cut the pepperoni in chunks. Place the chunks of pepperoni in a food processor fitted with the steel blade. Process for about 1 minute, until the pepperoni is minced. Add the mozzarella cubes. Process 20 to 30 seconds more until the mixture is finely minced. Transfer to a large mixing bowl.

3. Place the pound of skinless chicken in the food processor and process for 15 seconds. Add the eggs and process for another 30 seconds until a creamy, smooth paste is formed. Transfer to the bowl with the cheese and pepperoni mixture.

4. Dice the pepper halves into tiny squares, more or less uniform in size. Add the diced peppers to the mixing bowl. Using your hands, mix the peppers, chicken and egg paste, mozzarella, and pepperoni until well incorporated.

5. Divide this filling into five equal parts. Shape each fifth of filling so that it looks like a sausage.

6. Place each of the five whole chicken breasts in front of you, skin side down. Arrange a fifth of the filling across the middle of each breast. Fold each breast around the filling to close. Then transfer each chicken breast, seam side down, to an ungreased baking pan. Make sure to leave a little bit of space between each breast.

7. Pour the wine and the stock over the chicken. Cover the pan tightly with aluminum foil and bake in a 400-degree oven for 1 hour. When the chicken is cooked, turn the oven off to keep it warm while you make the sauce.

CHICKEN

5 *whole boneless chicken breasts with skin, each weighing about 1/2 pound*

1/2 *pound pepperoni*

1/2 *pound mozzarella cheese, cut in cubes*

1 *pound boneless chicken breasts without skin*

2 *eggs*

halves of 3 bell peppers—1 yellow, 1 red, 1 green

2 *cups white wine*

2 *cups chicken stock (canned or homemade)*

1. Bring the cooking liquid to a boil. Add the wine and whisk in the cornstarch to make the liquid smooth. Reduce the heat and then stir in the cheese. Simmer the sauce, uncovered, to desired thickness, about 10 minutes.

2. To serve, slice the chicken. Spoon a puddle of the sauce onto individual plates and arrange three slices of the chicken on top of the sauce.

SAUCE

All the cooking liquid from the chicken (see above)

1 cup white wine

3 tablespoons cornstarch

1/2 cup coarsely grated Parmesan cheese

CHICKEN PARMIGIANA

Serves 4–6

With the cheese oozing over the seasoned, succulent chicken like a thick blanket and the red sauce bathing all in a warm, slightly spicy red glow, this makes an especially inviting and satisfying meal.

1. In a large bowl, combine 1½ cups of the Romano with the bread crumbs, black pepper, garlic powder, and parsley. Using your hand, mix well. In a separate bowl, beat the eggs slightly.

2. Heat the oil in a skillet over medium high heat. Test the oil by throwing a pinch of the bread crumb mixture into the skillet. When the mixture browns quickly, the oil is ready to use.

3. Dip each piece of chicken first in the eggs and then in the bread crumb mixture. Place each coated chicken piece in the hot oil and fry until lightly browned on all sides.

4. Meanwhile, pour a third of the red sauce into a casserole dish. When the chicken is browned, transfer the pieces to the casserole. Pour another third of the sauce on top of the chicken. Arrange the mozzarella slices on top. Pour on the rest of the sauce. Sprinkle with the remaining ¼ cup of Romano.

5. Bake the chicken, uncovered, in a 400-degree oven for 20 minutes.

1¾ cups coarsely grated Romano cheese

1/2 cup plain bread crumbs

1 tablespoon coarsely ground black pepper

1 teaspoon garlic powder

1 cup coarsely chopped Italian parsley

3 eggs

1½ cups oil

3 chicken breasts, boned and skinned, each cut in half

2 cups Famous Tomato Sauce (see p. 69)

6 slices mozzarella cheese 1/8 inch thick

GRANDMOTHER'S ROAST STUFFED CHICKEN

Serves 4

The rosemary-flecked skin is crisp, the meat moist, and the stuffing inside this simply prepared chicken dish is bursting with flavor. Basting often is the secret to the crispy outside, and it's the salami inside that gives this stuffing that special bite.

1. In a large bowl, combine the eggs, Romano, salami, parsley, and coarse black pepper. Using your hand or a fork, mix thoroughly until the consistency of the stuffing is soft and moist.

2. Stuff the chicken, leaving the cavity open. Place the chicken in a roasting pan.

3. Sprinkle the outside of the chicken evenly with the salt first, followed by the fine black pepper and then the rosemary. Dot the chunks of butter randomly on top of the chicken. Pour 1/4 cup of water into the bottom of the pan.

4. Place the chicken in a 400-degree oven and bake for 2 hours until the skin gets golden brown and crispy. Baste from pan drippings on occasion and feel free to add more butter or water, if needed, after about an hour. When the chicken is done, the pan drippings can be spooned over it just before serving.

6 eggs, slightly beaten

3 cups coarsely grated Romano cheese

1/3 pound salami, sliced and diced in 1/2-inch cubes

1 cup coarsely chopped fresh Italian parsley

1 tablespoon coarsely ground black pepper

5-pound roasting chicken

1 heaping teaspoon salt

1 teaspoon finely ground black pepper

1 heaping tablespoon dried rosemary

4 tablespoons (1/2 stick) butter, cut in 1/2-inch chunks

1/4 cup water

BRAISED PHEASANT

Like other small game birds, pheasant, once considered a rare delicacy, is becoming more readily available in our supermarkets these days. When I was growing up in rural Pennsylvania, pheasant was never in short supply either, since people would go into the woods and hunt the birds. This recipe was a popular way to cook its mild-flavored white meat.

1. Heat the oil and butter together in a deep skillet or a Dutch oven.

2. Add the cut-up pheasant, salt, pepper, rosemary, garlic cloves, and bay leaf to the skillet. Cook over medium heat for 15 minutes or until the pheasant is browned.

3. Pour in the wine. Cover the skillet or Dutch oven, lower the heat, and continue to cook for 30 minutes or until the meat is tender. Remove bay leaf before serving.

1/4 cup olive oil

1/4 cup (1/2 stick) butter

4-pound pheasant cut into serving pieces

1 teaspoon salt

1 teaspoon coarsely ground black pepper

1 teaspoon dried rosemary leaves

2 garlic cloves, peeled and left whole

1 bay leaf

1/2 cup red wine

VEGETABLES HOT AND COLD

THERE IS NO LIMIT TO THE NUMBER OF WAYS YOU CAN EAT vegetables. Or so it seemed when I was a child and my family had only to go out to our garden to gather food for our table year-round. My grandmother would pick sun-ripened tomatoes at their peak and can them for future sauces; during the summer we ate salads made of our lettuce or sometimes dandelion greens; and as winter approached, my mother would simmer carrots, celery, and onions she had picked into nourishing soups. Eggplants were my father's specialty to cook with bread crumbs and grated cheese in his Sicilian style; we stuffed the artichokes and baked them according to a traditional recipe too, while the spinach was fried and served on sandwiches.

But to me the most impressive vegetable was the one that had sustained poverty-stricken Italians since the 1600s and that many Americans, as recently as a century ago, regarded as food fit only for animals. In our house, potatoes weren't held in particularly high esteem either, even though we ate them every way—mashed, baked, fried, boiled, and rolled into gnocchi. But I wasn't swayed by the potato's lowly reputation; for me, this plainest of vegetables could never be ordinary. That was because I had eaten potatoes the best way they could be eaten: at a potato roast.

A potato you had dug up yourself was all you needed to bring; a shallow hole surrounded by stones was always the predesignated location. In Republic, we kids held our roasts at night in the alleyway between my aunt's house and the funeral parlor. We got a good blaze going out of paper and twigs and then threw our potatoes into the fire. After about an hour and a half, when our talk and the flames were dying down, the roasting was over. With a stick, we each jabbed at a blackened potato and scraped off the charcoal. No matter how many of us there were huddled around the pit, somehow we always knew that the potato we were about to eat was the one we had found in our own garden.

Maybe it's because of the roasts that today I prefer my vegetables to be well cooked, and why I especially enjoy preparing any meal in which vegetables play a starring role. Of course, as I learned from my family, that role can take many forms, even for the same vegetable. Take, for example, Easy Marinated Mushrooms and baked Stuffed Mushrooms Italian Style, or Kiki's Baked Stuffed Eggplant and Eggplant Parmigiana. There is, after all, no proper way to cook vegetables, but there is a way to cook vegetables properly. And that is whether boiling, baking, sautéing, stuffing, steaming, mashing, mixing, or whatever to treat all vegetables as though they were a potato at a roast: with respect. ◆

KIKI'S BAKED STUFFED EGGPLANT

Serves 4–6

Hollowed eggplant shells make graceful receptacles for the soft, moist filling in this satisfying meatless main course. The recipe comes by way of my cousin Kiki, from her stepmother, Rosa, who has always been a wonderful cook.

1. Cut both eggplants in half lengthwise. Scoop out the pulp of the eggplants, leaving 1/2 inch around the edges. Dice the pulp fine and place it in a large bowl.

2. Add the tomatoes and a little of their juice, the minced garlic, Parmesan, pepper, bread crumbs, and chopped parsley to the bowl. Mix together thoroughly. Add more tomato juice if necessary to produce a soft, moist filling.

3. Pack and mound the filling into the four eggplant halves. (You might have some filling left over.) Place the stuffed eggplant halves in a baking dish.

4. Pour 1/4 cup of the oil over each eggplant half, then bake in a 400-degree oven for 1 1/2 hours.

2 large eggplants

2 pounds 3 ounces (1 large can) peeled whole tomatoes, with some juice reserved

2 very large or 4 medium garlic cloves, peeled and minced

2 cups coarsely grated Parmesan cheese

1 tablespoon coarsely ground black pepper

1 cup plain bread crumbs

1 bunch coarsely chopped Italian parsley

1 cup oil

SICILIAN EGGPLANT

Serves 4–6

I named this recipe as I did because this is my Sicilian father's well-seasoned way of layering and cooking eggplant. But the name does not give you license, as my husband Cosmo jokes, to stick a knife in the eggplant before baking it.

1. Mix together the Romano, bread crumbs, black pepper, and parsley.

2. Peel the eggplant and then slice it thin, lengthwise.

3. To assemble, arrange a layer of eggplant slices across the bottom of a 9 × 13 × 2-inch baking pan. Sprinkle 1/2 cup of the cheese and bread-crumb mixture over the layer of eggplant and drizzle 1/2 cup of the oil over it.

4. Repeat each layer, in the same order, three more times.

5. Bake the eggplant in a 400-degree oven for 1 hour.

1 1/2 cups coarsely grated Romano cheese

1/2 cup plain bread crumbs

1 tablespoon coarsely ground black pepper

1 tablespoon coarsely chopped Italian parsley

1 large eggplant

2 cups oil

EGGPLANT PARMIGIANA

You can order eggplant parmigiana in almost any Italian restaurant. But I think it's only fair to warn you that once you've made our version of this popular dish, the best eggplant parmigiana you'll ever eat will be your own.

1. Cut the green ends off both eggplants and slice them in 1/2-inch circles. Set aside.

2. Heat the oil in a skillet. Meanwhile, beat the eggs, along with a little bit of water, in a shallow dish. Place the flour in a separate shallow dish.

3. Dip each eggplant circle into the egg mixture and then into the flour, making sure to coat well on both sides.

4. Fry in the hot oil until both sides are golden. Drain the fried eggplant on paper towels and set aside.

5. To assemble, cover the bottom of a 9 × 12 × 2-inch baking pan with some tomato sauce. Arrange a layer of the eggplant over the sauce, fitting the eggplant slices tightly together like a puzzle. Cover the eggplant with more sauce. Arrange a layer of mozzarella over this. Top the mozzarella with more sauce.

6. Repeat these layers twice.

7. Sprinkle the Romano over the top and bake the eggplant in a 400-degree oven for 30 minutes.

2 large eggplants

3 cups oil

4 eggs

1/4 cup water

4 cups flour

6 cups Famous Tomato Sauce (see p. 69)

16 slices mozzarella cheese, 1/4 inch thick

1 cup coarsely grated Romano cheese

STUFFED RED PEPPERS

This compact and colorful one-dish meal, from an old family recipe, proves both nutritious and surprisingly satisfying. Be sure to cook the peppers until the tops become partially black and crispy. This is what gives the stuffing a subtle roasted flavor.

1. Using a sharp knife, core the six peppers. The cavities can be wide, but be sure to leave each pepper whole.

2. In a large bowl, combine the lean ground beef, rice, onions, and 1 cup of the tomato sauce with 2 cups of the Romano and all the pine nuts and currants. Season with the black and red pepper. With your hands or a fork (I prefer using my hands), mix thoroughly.

3. Spoon a mound of this mixture into the cavity of each pepper. Stuff tightly and fill each pepper to the brim.

4. Lay each stuffed pepper down on its side in a shallow roasting pan. Pour the remaining tomato sauce over the peppers. Pour the water into the bottom of the pan. Sprinkle the salt and the remaining cheese evenly over the peppers.

5. Bake the peppers, uncovered, in a 450-degree oven for 1½ hours. The meat and rice will cook perfectly inside their pepper beds.

6 *large red bell peppers (or green if red are unavailable)*

2 *pounds lean ground beef*

1½ *cups uncooked rice*

3 *heaping tablespoons dried minced onions*

4 *cups tomato sauce (canned is fine)*

3 *cups coarsely grated Romano cheese*

½ *cup pine nuts*

½ *cup currants or golden raisins*

2 *heaping teaspoons coarsely ground black pepper*

1 *teaspoon crushed red pepper*

1 *cup water*

1 *tablespoon salt*

MEATLESS STUFFED PEPPERS

Serves 4–6

When they're cooked, the outsides of these peppers become soft and wrinkled. This unusual appearance makes my friend Gilda's simple, easy-to-vary recipe all the more appealing.

1. Using a sharp knife, core the peppers, making sure to leave them whole.

2. In a bowl, combine the bread, parsley, pressed garlic, chopped olives, diced mushrooms, salt, pepper, and Romano. Pour in the oil, a little at a time. Using your hands, mix thoroughly. As the bread absorbs the oil, the entire filling should become soft and moist.

3. Pack the filling, not too tightly, into the cavity of each pepper. Rub the outside of the peppers with the oil remaining on your hands. Place the peppers in a baking pan and set the pan, uncovered, in a 350-degree oven. Bake for 35 minutes, until the peppers are cooked through.

VARIATION: Add 1 small can anchovies, mashed, and 2–3 tablespoons pine nuts to the filling. If you make this variation, you should have enough filling for 6 peppers.

4 *long green Italian peppers*

3 *cups coarsely chopped Italian bread (preferably a day old), white part only*

3 *tablespoons coarsely chopped Italian parsley*

4 *garlic cloves, peeled and pressed*

4 1/4 *ounces (1 can) pitted black olives, finely chopped*

3 *large mushrooms, diced*

1 *pinch salt*

1 *pinch coarsely ground black pepper*

2 *tablespoons coarsely grated Romano cheese*

2/3 *cup oil*

STUFFED TOMATOES

Serves 6

My friend Joe likes to say, "You can throw money away, but never food." That's one of the reasons Joe likes his wife Gilda to make her stuffed tomatoes, an attractive and tasty side dish in which nothing is wasted.

1. Preheat oven to 350 degrees F.

2. Slice ½ inch off the top of each tomato. Set these tomato caps aside. (Try to remember which cap goes with which tomato—it will make a nicer presentation later.) Using a teaspoon, core out the pulp from each of the tomatoes. Place the pulp, including seeds, in a mixing bowl.

3. Mash the tomato pulp until it is practically all juice. Add the mint and basil. With a garlic press, add the garlic. Mix in the uncooked rice, salt, pepper, oil, diced celery, and Romano. Continue to mix until this filling is well incorporated.

4. Pack the filling tightly into the shell of each tomato. Cover each filled tomato with its cap. Arrange the stuffed tomatoes in a baking dish so that they're almost touching. Pour the water, along with any leftover filling, into the bottom of the dish.

5. Cover the dish tightly with aluminum foil and place it in the preheated oven. Bake for at least an hour, until the rice is cooked a golden brown and is swelling over the sides of the tomatoes.

6 *very ripe tomatoes (preferably with stems)*

1 *tablespoon fresh mint*

1 *tablespoon fresh basil or 1 pinch dry basil*

3 *garlic cloves, peeled*

1½ *cups uncooked rice*

1 *pinch salt*

1 *pinch coarsely ground black pepper*

2 *tablespoons oil*

1 *small celery stalk, diced very fine*

2 *tablespoons coarsely grated Romano cheese*

¾ *cup water*

GRANDMOTHER'S BAKED TOMATOES

Serves 4–6

When the huge, hot sun-baked tomatoes in our garden were at their peak of ripeness, this is how we often served them.

1. Place the tomato halves, face up, in a baking dish. Sprinkle the salt, pepper, minced garlic, and parsley over the tomatoes. Then drizzle on the oil.

2. Bake the tomatoes in a 400-degree oven for 1 hour.

4 large ripe tomatoes, cut in half

1/2 teaspoon salt

1/2 teaspoon coarsely ground black pepper

4 large garlic cloves, peeled and minced

1 teaspoon finely chopped Italian parsley

8 tablespoons oil

STUFFED ARTICHOKES

Serves 6

I wasn't surprised to read that in Italian marketplaces artichokes are often artistically displayed like flowers. Whenever I trim the vegetable according to this old Sicilian recipe, their lovely shapes remind me of roses. Learning how to cut the stem of the artichoke so that the core, which holds the leaves together, remains intact is easy once you get the hang of it. Besides, once you taste these "flowers" filled, you'll be glad you put in that little bit of extra effort.

1. Turn each artichoke on its side. Holding the artichoke firmly by its leaves, slice the stem off the bottom with a serrated knife, being careful not to cut into the leaves. (Your artichokes should now be able to sit flat on your work surface.) Then slice about an inch off the top of each artichoke. Using a scissors, trim the tips off all the artichoke leaves.

2. In a large pot, bring 8 quarts of water to a boil and drop in the artichokes. Cover the pot tightly with a lid and boil on high heat for 30 to 35 minutes until the artichokes are semi-tender and have lost most of their green color. Meanwhile, mix the ingredients for the stuffing.

6 artichokes

2 cups coarsely chopped Italian parsley

1 heaping teaspoon coarsely ground black pepper

2 cups unseasoned bread crumbs

3 cups coarsely grated Romano cheese

1 teaspoon garlic powder or 3 large garlic cloves, chopped very fine

3 cups oil

3. Combine the parsley, black pepper, bread crumbs, Romano, and garlic in a bowl. Mix well by hand.

4. When the artichokes are cooked, place them upside down to drain and cool slightly. Then open the leaves. Starting from the outside leaves and working to the center, sprinkle in the stuffing.

Holding the artichoke in one hand, sprinkle the stuffing in between the leaves with the other hand.

5. Place each stuffed artichoke upright in a baking pan. Drizzle 1/2 cup of oil over each artichoke so that the oil seeps into the stuffing.

6. Bake the artichokes in a 400-degree oven for 30 to 40 minutes until they are slightly browned on top.

ITALIAN VEGETABLE ROAST

Serves 4–6

The large sizes of the vegetables and the array of their colors make this an especially beautiful-looking dish. If we had thought of cooking all these vegetables together when we were kids we might never have been satisfied with roasting just potatoes.

1. Place all the vegetables in a mixing bowl. Add the oil, herbs, and seasoning. Mix well so that all the vegetables are coated.

2. Pour the vegetable mixture into a 9 × 12-inch baking pan, spreading the vegetables uniformly across the bottom of the pan. Roast the vegetables for 45 minutes to 1 hour, turning them every fifteen minutes.

3 bell peppers—1 red, 1 yellow, 1 green, cored, seeded, and quartered

3 Italian eggplants, quartered lengthwise

1 large head garlic, unpeeled and separated into cloves

2 baby zucchini, quartered lengthwise

2 baby yellow squash, quartered lengthwise

1 large yellow onion, peeled and quartered

1 cup olive oil

1 tablespoon dried oregano

1 tablespoon dried basil

1 tablespoon dried thyme

1 tablespoon coarsely ground black pepper

2 teaspoons salt

FRIED FRESH SPINACH

Serves 4–6

1. Heat the oil in a large skillet or a Dutch oven over medium high heat. Place the spinach in the oil and begin to fry.

2. Add the salt, garlic powder, black pepper, and red pepper. Continue to fry until the spinach is wilted. Serve with fresh Italian bread.

1/2 cup oil

30 ounces (3 packages) fresh spinach, washed

1 teaspoon salt

2 teaspoons garlic powder

1 teaspoon coarsely ground black pepper

1/2 teaspoon crushed red pepper (optional)

ROASTED HERBED POTATOES

This way of preparing potatoes, a kind of adult version of our childhood roasts, is simply great.

1. Place the unpeeled potatoes in a large bowl. Sprinkle on all the seasonings. Coat with the oil and stir thoroughly.

2. Place the potatoes in a shallow baking dish and bake in a 400-degree oven for 1 hour.

12 *new red-skinned potatoes, cut in half*

1/2 *teaspoon salt*

1/2 *teaspoon coarsely ground black pepper*

1/2 *teaspoon thyme*

1 *large garlic clove, peeled and minced*

1 *teaspoon dried parsley flakes*

1/4 *teaspoon garlic powder*

1/3 *cup olive oil*

MALONE

This is, without a doubt, the most fabulous mashed potato dish I've ever eaten. It's amazing that something this healthful could be so unbelievably rich.

1. Place the potatoes in a pot and cover them with water. Bring the water to a boil over high heat. Lower the heat and cook until the potatoes are fork-tender, about 20 minutes.

2. Drain half the water from the pot. Place the spinach on top of the potatoes, cover the pot, and continue to boil the remaining water for 5 more minutes until the spinach is wilted. Remove the pot from the heat and drain. Leave the vegetables in the pot.

3. Add the half-and-half, garlic, butter, salt, and pepper to the potatoes and spinach in the pot.

4. Mash all the ingredients in the pot with a metal hand masher until the mixture is just slightly lumpy.

5. Transfer the mixture to a large casserole dish (or individual casserole dishes if you have them) and sprinkle with the Parmesan. Serve immediately.

1 1/2 *pounds new potatoes, unpeeled (about 10 potatoes)*

1 *pound fresh spinach, washed*

1/3 *cup half-and-half or light cream*

3 *large garlic cloves, peeled and chopped*

1/4 *cup (1/2 stick) butter*

1/2 *teaspoon salt*

1/2 *teaspoon pepper*

1/4 *cup coarsely grated Parmesan cheese*

CIAMBOTTA

This delightful jumble of vegetables is at home in any setting. My friends Gilda and Joe, whose recipe this is, like to eat it hot, along with a meat, but ciambotta is just as enjoyable when served cold, as the main course at a lively summertime picnic or al fresco luncheon.

1. Squash the tomatoes with your hands or a fork into a saucepan.

2. Combine the oil, minced garlic, salt, pepper, and chopped parsley with the squashed tomatoes in the saucepan. Stir. Cook, covered, on low heat for 45 minutes to 1 hour until the sauce thickens.

3. Meanwhile, place the potatoes in a pot and cover them with water. Bring the water to a boil and cook about 20 to 25 minutes, until the potatoes are tender enough to be easily pierced by the tip of a knife. Drain, cut the potatoes in chunks, and set them aside.

4. When the sauce has thickened, add the pepperoni and mushrooms. With the heat still on low, stir and, with the saucepan still covered, cook together for 15 minutes.

5. Add the pepper strips and the sliced onions to the mixture in the saucepan. Stir and cook for 10 more minutes.

6. Add the zucchini and the potatoes to the saucepan. Stir and cook for 10 additional minutes.

12 ounces (1 can) peeled whole tomatoes, with juice

2 tablespoons oil

2 garlic cloves, peeled and minced

1 pinch salt

1 pinch coarsely ground black pepper

1 tablespoon coarsely chopped Italian parsley

2 large potatoes, peeled

1/4 pound pepperoni, sliced thin

1/4 pound fresh mushrooms, sliced

1 green pepper, cored, seeded, and sliced in thin strips

1 medium yellow onion, peeled and sliced

2 zucchini, cut in 3/4-inch slices

FLORENCE UMBERGER'S ANTIPASTO

Most antipastos consist of little more than a few pieces of salami and prosciutto. With this wonderful vegetable salad, my friend Florence brought a whole new meaning to the word.

Place all the ingredients in a large bowl and mix well. Serve or refrigerate.

4 cups (1/2 bunch) celery, cut in 1/2-inch pieces

6 ounces (1 can) pitted black olives

2 cups green olives stuffed with pimentos (slice 1 cup into thirds)

2 cups roasted sweet red peppers (jarred or canned), cut in 1/4-inch strips

1 small red onion, peeled and sliced

1/2 cup capers

1 cup olive oil

1/2 cup red wine vinegar

1 teaspoon salt

1 teaspoon coarsely ground black pepper

1 teaspoon garlic powder

EASY MARINATED MUSHROOMS

The zing of fresh lemon almost steals the spotlight in this easy-to-prepare appetizer or side dish.

1. Slice each mushroom into three or four chunks. Place the mushroom chunks in a large mixing bowl and set aside.

2. Pour the oil into a separate bowl. Whisk in all the remaining ingredients.

3. Pour the marinade over the mushrooms and mix thoroughly. Cover the bowl and refrigerate for at least 8 hours, turning often.

1 pound fresh mushrooms

3/4 cup oil

1 1/2 teaspoons grated lemon peel

1/4 cup freshly squeezed lemon juice

1 heaping teaspoon dried oregano

1 heaping teaspoon garlic salt

1/4 teaspoon coarsely ground black pepper

CAULIFLOWER VINAIGRETTE

Serves 4–6

1. Cut the cauliflower into quarters and place it in a large pot. Cover the cauliflower with water and bring to a boil. Lower the heat, cover the pot, and simmer until the cauliflower is soft enough to be easily pierced with the tines of a fork (about 20 minutes). Drain and let cool.

2. Meanwhile, combine all the rest of the ingredients in a glass or plastic container fitted with a lid. Cover and shake well.

3. Cut each cauliflower quarter in half (or smaller pieces if you'd like). Transfer the cooled cauliflower to a serving bowl. Pour the dressing over the cauliflower and serve cold or slightly warm.

1 head cauliflower, including green stalks

1/2 cup olive oil

1 teaspoon salt

1 teaspoon coarsely ground black pepper

4 garlic cloves, minced fine

1/4 cup wine vinegar

1/2 cup coarsely chopped Italian parsley

STUFFED MUSHROOMS ITALIAN STYLE

Serves 4 as an appetizer

This delicious filling refrigerates, and even freezes, nicely if you find you have some left over after your mushrooms are stuffed.

1. Remove the caps from all the mushrooms and scoop them out with a teaspoon. Do not wash the caps, though you may want to wipe them with a damp cloth or paper towel. Set them aside.

2. Place the stems in a food processor fitted with the steel blade. Process the mushroom stems until fine.

3. Melt the butter in a skillet over medium high heat. Add the chopped stems and the garlic and sauté for about 1 minute.

4. Remove the skillet from the heat and add the rest of the ingredients. Mix well, then stuff each mushroom cap with the mixture.

5. Preheat the broiler to 400 degrees. Place the stuffed mushrooms on the low rack under the broiler and, watching continuously, broil for 5 minutes or until the stuffing turns golden. Garnish with pimento strips, if you'd like, and serve.

12 large mushrooms, 3 inches in diameter if possible, **or** *24 smaller mushrooms*

3/4 pound (3 sticks) butter

4 garlic cloves, minced

2 cups unseasoned bread crumbs

1/2 teaspoon coarsely ground black pepper

1/2 cup coarsely grated Romano cheese

1/2 cup chopped Italian parsley

Juice of 1 lemon

Pimento strips for garnish (optional)

MOZZARELLA DI BUFALA INSALATA

Serves 4–6

Recent summer visitors to Italy have come back raving about this delicacy, which they had in restaurants. They also returned with questions about how buffalo mozzarella salad is served. I investigated and this is what I discovered.

1. Slice the mozzarella and the tomatoes in 1/2-inch pieces. (Or you can wedge the tomatoes, if you prefer.)

2. Alternating the pieces, arrange the tomatoes and mozzarella on a serving platter.

3. Break the fresh basil into pieces with your hands or cut it with a pair of scissors. Sprinkle the fresh basil, or whichever herb you are using, over the top of the tomatoes and mozzarella.

4. Drizzle on the olive oil. Add salt and pepper and serve or refrigerate.

1 1/2 *pounds buffalo mozzarella cheese*

2 *large beefsteak tomatoes* **or** *4 plum tomatoes*

1 *cup fresh basil leaves* **or** *1 tablespoon dried basil* **or** *1 teaspoon oregano*

1/3 *cup olive oil*

Salt to taste

Coarsely ground black pepper

SPINACH SALAD

Serves 4–6

1. Break up the spinach to larger than bite-sized pieces. Slice each artichoke heart in half, or quarters if you'd prefer.

2. Combine the spinach, artichoke hearts (including marinade), almonds, croutons, and Cheddar cheese in a salad bowl. Dress with the lemon juice and wine vinegar. Toss well and serve.

10 *ounces (1 package) fresh spinach, washed*

8 1/2 *ounces (1 large jar or can) artichoke hearts in marinade*

1/2 *cup sliced or slivered almonds*

1 *cup croutons (any flavor)*

1 1/2 *cups shredded Cheddar cheese*

Juice of 2 lemons

2 *tablespoons wine vinegar*

VINAIGRETTE WITH PESTO

Makes 1–1¼ cups

Oil and vinegar will never be the same.

1. Combine the oil with all the other ingredients in a container fitted with a tight lid. Shake well and serve.

¾ cup oil

2 tablespoons red wine vinegar

½ heaping teaspoon coarsely ground black pepper

¼ teaspoon garlic powder

1 teaspoon salt

1½ tablespoons pesto (see p. 75) or 1 heaping teaspoon dried basil plus 3 small garlic cloves, peeled and minced, 1 heaping tablespoon coarsely grated Parmesan cheese, and 1 teaspoon pine nuts

CHEDDAR-WALNUT DRESSING

Makes 1¼–1½ cups dressing

The sharpness of the Cheddar shavings blend beautifully with the smooth nuttiness of the walnut oil in this unusual dressing.

1. Place the oils, vinegar, and egg yolk in a mixing bowl. Whisk together.

2. Add the mustard, salt, and pepper. Whisk again.

3. Fold in the Cheddar cheese and the walnuts.

¼ cup walnut oil

½ cup regular oil

¼ cup red wine vinegar

1 egg yolk

1 tablespoon Dijon-style prepared mustard

1 teaspoon salt

½ teaspoon white pepper

⅓ cup coarsely grated sharp Cheddar cheese

⅓ cup ground walnuts

DESSERTS

I NEVER SAW A BAKERY UNTIL MY FAMILY MOVED TO MASSACHU-
setts. I never tasted a pastry filled with cream. Cookies were the Italian ones
my Aunt Eleanore made once a year, at Christmastime and stored, covered
with newspapers, in a cold back room. No wonder we so appreciated the
homemade chocolate or vanilla batter topped with her "seven-minute frosting" that my mother baked for birthdays: they were our only cakes. There
was, of course, fried dough that we dipped in sugar, semisweet breads, and the
Mary Janes we bought at Serreta's candy store, and little wax bottles we
chewed like gum after we bit off the tops and sucked out the syrup. But the
only real dessert we had, regularly and in abundance, was fruit.

Plums, peaches, pears, cherries, grapes and more—any fruit that could be
grown in the hills of Pennsylvania was there for the picking in our garden. The
apples were carried up to the attic every autumn where, staying dry, they
lasted through the winter; most of the other fruit was cut in half and preserved
in a simple syrup of sugar and water. Hucksters drove up in their broken-
down trucks to sell us watermelons, bananas, oranges, cantaloupes, and other
fresh sweets from tropical climates. And during the summer my cousin Kiki
and I would scavenge the bushes in nearby fields until our hands were stained
a deep and seemingly permanent purple, and the thorns had scratched our
bare legs and arms as we gathered wild blackberries that my mother would
bake in double-crust pies.

Having known only such simple sweetness, I was unprepared for the rich
allure of desserts, their darker side. Wandering the streets of Boston's North
End as a teenager, I was easily seduced by marzipan, many-layered chocolate
and rum cakes, or any dessert waiting in a window on which I could feast my
eyes. But almost every time I succumbed to my urges, I was disappointed. The

pastry tasted commercial to me, the fillings artificial. Still captivated by their beauty, I resolved to learn to make many of these desserts myself. It was a decision I've never regretted, despite the work. Once you've eaten a home-made dessert like cannoli, you just can't buy it anymore. ◆

pastries

PIZZELLES

Makes 24 pizzelles

These cookies, which look like miniature waffles, couldn't be easier to make once you've purchased a pizzelle iron at an Italian import store. Just be sure to make plenty of them because you probably won't have the chance to see how beautifully pizzelles keep in a plastic bag or big glass jar when these cookies disappear in no time!

1. Combine the beaten eggs, sugar, cooled butter, and anise seed (or other flavoring) in a bowl. Stir until the sugar is dissolved. In another bowl, combine the flour and baking powder, then add to the egg and sugar mixture.

2. Heat the pizzelle iron.

3. Using two tablespoonfuls for each, make two balls of dough. Place both balls inside the iron and press down. If you're using an electric iron, cook 1 to 2 minutes, or until the steam stops and the cookies are golden brown. If your iron is hand-held, cook over medium-high heat on either a gas or electric stove for 2 minutes.

4. Repeat step 3 until you have used up all the dough.

3 eggs, beaten

1 cup sugar

1/2 cup butter, melted then cooled

2 teaspoons anise seed, anise extract, vanilla extract, or orange extract

3 1/2 cups flour

2 tablespoons baking powder

ITALIAN COOKIES OR LITTLE CAKES

Wherever there is an Italian celebration, be it a baby shower, holiday, or wedding, you'll find these festive treats given a position of importance in the center of the dessert table.

1. Cream the sugar and shortening together in a large bowl. Using an electric mixer, beat in the eggs, one at a time. Continuing to beat, add the extract.

2. In a separate bowl, mix the flour with the salt and baking powder. Combine this dry mixture with the creamed one. The dough should now be soft, but not super sticky.

3. Using your hands, make round balls about 2 inches across. Place each ball on an ungreased cookie sheet and bake in a 400-degree oven for 12 to 15 minutes, or until the cookies are very light brown. While the cookies cool, make the frosting. (The cookies must be really cool before you frost them.)

COOKIES

3/4 cup sugar

1/2 cup shortening

5 eggs

1 teaspoon lemon or anise extract or 1/2 teaspoon vanilla extract plus 1/2 teaspoon almond extract

3 1/2 cups flour

Pinch salt

4 teaspoons baking powder

1. Mix the sugar and flavoring together in a bowl. Add the milk, 2 tablespoons at a time, until the frosting is a spreading consistency, not runny but slightly stiff.

2. When the cookies are cold, use a butter knife to spread the frosting on top.

3. Dip each frosted cookies into the colored sprinkles or nonpareilles.

FROSTING

1 cup confectioners' sugar

1 teaspoon of whatever flavoring you used in the dough

Milk, as needed

1 cup colored sprinkles or nonpareilles

ANISE BISCOTTI — Not Like Nonnie's but good, easier.

1. Preheat the oven to 375 degrees. Butter and flour a 4-inch-wide loaf pan.

2. Place the eggs and sugar in a bowl and beat well with an electric mixer for 5 minutes.

3. Add the flour and, turning the mixer to a low setting, blend gently and thoroughly. Continuing to blend, add the anise seeds.

4. Pour the batter into the loaf* pan and bake for 20 minutes. ✳ Use 8×8 sq.

5. Remove the pan from the oven, but leave the oven on. Remove the loaf from the pan. Cut the loaf into angled slices 1 inch thick.

6. Place the slices on their sides on a cookie sheet and return them to the oven. Brown the slices on one side for 5 minutes. Then turn the slices over and brown them for 5 minutes on the other side. Let cool and serve.

12/25/90

Butter for greasing
Flour for dusting
2 eggs
3/4 cup sugar
1¼ cups flour
2 teaspoons anise seeds✳

✳ Extract & slivered almonds, toasted.

BISCOTTI DI PRATO

One of the most popular Italian biscuits.

1. Mix together the flour, sugar, baking powder, and salt in a large stainless steel bowl. Add the eggs and, using your hands, mix again until a dough forms. If the dough is sticky, add more flour. Add the nuts and knead for 5 minutes.

2. Turn the dough out onto a floured surface. Divide the dough into four pieces. Roll each piece into ropes measuring about 17 inches long and 3/4 inch in diameter.

3. Place the ropes on two buttered and floured cookie sheets. Brush the tops of the ropes with the beaten egg white.

4. Bake the ropes at 350 degrees for 25 to 30 minutes. Remove them from the oven and lower the temperature to 300 degrees.

5. Slice each rope into pieces each 1/2 to 3/4 inch thick. Place each piece on its side on the cookie sheet and bake until toasted, but not browned, about 25 to 30 minutes.

6. Remove the biscotti from the oven and cool them on a cooling rack. Serve and store the rest in a loosely covered container.

2 *cups flour*
3 1/4 *cups sugar*
1/2 *teaspoon baking powder*
  Pinch of salt
2 *eggs, beaten*
3/4 *cup toasted almonds (1/4 cup finely ground; 1/2 cup coarsely chopped)*
  Flour for dusting
  Butter for greasing
1 *egg white, beaten*

STRUFOLI

Serves 4–6

These tiny balls, deep-fried, honey-coated, and piled in cone and cluster shapes, are often used as a centerpiece on Christmas Day. I first made strufoli when my daughter was in second grade and the parents were asked to bring in a dish for an ethnic foods celebration. As I watched the children pulling off the sticky candy-covered balls from the huge mound and loving every minute of it, I found it hard to imagine anything sweeter.

1. In a food processor fitted with the steel blade, process the flour, salt, and eggs for 15 seconds.

2. Stop the machine, add the vanilla, and process for 5 seconds.

3. Turn the dough out on your work surface and knead a few times until you have shaped the dough into a small loaf. Slice the loaf into pieces 1/2 inch thick.

4. Roll each piece into a rope that is slightly thicker than a pencil. Slice each rope into pieces 1/2 inch long.

5. Heat the oil in an 8-inch skillet over high heat. Place as many pieces of dough in the skillet as will float uncrowded in one layer. (Cover the rest of the dough with a bowl to prevent drying out.) Fry the dough until golden brown. Remove the dough balls with a slotted spoon and drain on paper towels.

6. Repeat step 5 until you have fried all the dough.

7. Place the sugar and honey in a small saucepan and heat, stirring, over a low flame until the sugar dissolves, about 3 minutes.

8. Transfer the fried dough balls to a large bowl. Pour the dissolved sugar and honey over the balls. Stir carefully, making sure that all the balls are well coated.

9. Mound the balls on another plate. Sprinkle the top of the mound generously with colored sprinkles. Leave uncovered.

2 cups flour
1/4 teaspoon salt
3 eggs
1/2 teaspoon vanilla extract
2 cups oil
1 tablespoon sugar
1 cup honey
Colored sprinkles or non-pareilles for decoration

GRAPES GALORE

A cool and enticing finale to any important occasion, Grapes Galore looks great in anything from small clay bowls to delicate long-stemmed wineglasses. It tastes terrific the day you make it and, if possible, even better the next. What's more, if you have the crème fraîche ready, this memorable dessert takes less than five minutes to prepare.

Pour the port into the crème fraîche. Whisk in the powdered sugar. Gently fold in the grapes and pecans. Transfer the Grapes Galore to a serving bowl and chill for several hours before serving.

- 4 cups Crème Fraîche (see below)
- 8 tablespoons port
- 3/4 cup powdered sugar
- 2 pounds seedless white or red grapes, or a combination
- 1 1/2 cups pecan halves

In a large mixing bowl, whisk the heavy cream and the sour cream together. Cover loosely with plastic wrap and let stand at room temperature for at least 8 hours or until the crème fraîche begins to thicken and its tart flavor starts to develop.

CRÈME FRAÎCHE

- 2 cups heavy cream (not ultra-pasteurized)
- 2 cups sour cream

CANNOLI

You can't judge a cannoli by appearance alone. If you did, you might think that there was only one "correct" cannoli filling or that learning to shape the graceful cannoli shells requires years of training. In fact, the fillings are fun to invent and the shells easy to shape once you have the forms. Still, this doesn't minimize your feeling of accomplishment whenever you make your own cannoli.

1. In a food processor fitted with the steel blade, combine the flour, sugar, butter, egg, and 3 tablespoons of the Madeira. Process until the ingredients form a dough with a moist crumbly texture. Then add the other 3 tablespoons of Madeira and process for 15 seconds more.

2. Transfer the dough to a bowl and squeeze it together until the dough forms a ball. Cut the ball into quarters. Let the other quarters of dough rest under an inverted bowl to avoid drying out while you work with one quarter at a time.

3. With a rolling pin, roll out one quarter of dough to about 1/4 inch thickness. Using a 3-inch round biscuit or cookie cutter if you have one, or a glass measuring 3 inches in diameter, cut circles out of the dough.

4. With a rolling pin, roll each circle into a slightly larger circle measuring 3½ inches in diameter. Prepare six of these circles at a time.

5. Wrap each of the six circles of dough around a cannoli form. Using your fingers dampened with little bit of water, press the two closest edges of the dough together to seal. (Don't press too firmly; if you do, it will be difficult to remove the cooked shell from the form.)

6. Heat the oil in a skillet over medium high heat. Gently place the forms in the oil and fry, turning to brown all sides of the shells.

7. Remove the cooked shells from the skillet by grasping each one with a pair of tongs. Then, with the back of a spoon, gently push the cooked shell off the form and onto paper towels to cool.

8. Repeat steps 3 through 7 with the other quarters of dough. Then prepare one of the cannoli fillings given below.

VARIATION: You can make larger shells by using a

SHELLS

1¾ *cups flour*

  2 *tablespoons sugar*

  2 *tablespoons butter*

  1 *egg*

  6 *tablespoons Madeira wine or port*

    Water

  2 *cups oil*

  6 *metal cannoli forms (each 4 inches long)*

larger biscuit cutter or glass to cut circles. Any shells that come apart make wonderful snacks when dusted with powdered sugar.

In a bowl, whisk the first three ingredients together to a creamy consistency. (You can use a food processor, if you'd like, as long as you do not let the filling become too thin.) Remove the mixture from the processor and stir in the citron, if you're including it, by hand.

In a bowl, combine all the filling ingredients except the chocolate chips and whisk to a creamy consistency. Then add the chocolate chips.

Place the filling in a pastry bag fitted with a nozzle small enough to fit into the cannoli. Fill one end of each cannoli and then the other. Dust each filled cannoli with powdered sugar.

VARIATION: Coarsely chop pistachio nuts and add them to the filling or sprinkle them on the ends of the filled cannoli.

RICOTTA FILLING
- *2 pounds ricotta cheese*
- *2 teaspoons vanilla extract*
- *1½ cups confectioners' sugar*
- *¼ cup candied citron (optional)*

MASCARPONE FILLING
- *1 pound mascarpone cheese*
- *2 cups confectioners' sugar*
- *3 tablespoons vodka*
- *3 tablespoons Cointreau*
- *¼ cup mini-chocolate chips*

ASSEMBLY
- *Powdered sugar for dusting*

ZABAGLIONE

Serves 4–6

This rich wine dessert has become an international favorite. I like to serve it with not-too-sweet cookies.

1. Place the egg yolks and sugar in the top of a double boiler and beat with an electric mixer until the mixture is thick and lemon-colored.

2. Stir in the Marsala and set over simmering water. Continue to beat constantly with the mixer until the mixture begins to thicken and coats a spoon.

3. When the mixture starts to rise to the top of the pot, remove it from the heat. Pour the zabaglione into individual wineglasses and serve hot or chilled.

6 egg yolks
½ cup sugar
1 cup Marsala wine

SWEET CHOCOLATE LASAGNA

Serves 4–6 or even more

Over the years I've explained that my chocolate macaroni is usually meant to be served as a first or main course more times than I care to remember. But one day, in an adventurous mood, I decided to further explore the sweeter side of the cocoa-pasta connection the way many of our customers, and maybe nature itself, intended. This luscious lasagna is where my adventure led.

1. In a food processor fitted with the steel blade, combine the cocoa, flour, and eggs. Process until the dough forms a ball or a layer. If the dough seems too dry, add water a teaspoon at a time, and reprocess. If the dough seems too sticky, add more flour, a tablespoon at a time, and reprocess. (For more information, see p. 00.)

2. Turn the dough out onto a lightly floured surface and form the dough into a nice, neat ball.

3. Roll the dough into a rough circle or oval as thick as a nickel and about 2 feet in diameter.

4. Fold the circle or oval like a jelly roll. Cut strands of macaroni the width of lasagna noodles.

5. Bring 5 quarts of water to a boil, drop in the lasagna, and stir. When the water returns to a boil, cook the lasagna for 1 minute. Rinse in very cold water, drain, and set aside.

CHOCOLATE MACARONI
1/3 cup sweetened cocoa (I use Ghirardelli)
2 cups flour
3 eggs

1. Combine the ricotta, powdered sugar, and Cointreau in the food processor with the steel blade. Process just until the mixture is smooth.

2. Prepare to layer the lasagna in an extra-deep lasagna pan. Place three strips of lasagna across the bottom of the pan, making sure the strips overlap a little. Spread 1 cup of the ricotta mixture over the lasagna. Sprinkle on the pistachios. Layer on three more strips of lasagna followed by another cup of the ricotta mixture. Place half the can of mandarin oranges over this. Layer on three more strips of lasagna, followed by another cup of the ricotta mixture. Sprinkle all the chocolate chips on next. Add three more strips of lasagna and a final cup of the ricotta mixture as the last layer.

RICOTTA FILLING
4 cups ricotta
3/4 cup powdered sugar
1/3 cup Cointreau
1 can (11 ounces) mandarin oranges, drained, or raspberries or strawberries in season
1/3 cup chocolate chips
3 tablespoons shelled, unsalted pistachios, coarsely chopped
Italian wild cherries in heavy syrup, or some other fruit for garnish

3. Decorate the top of your lasagna with the remaining mandarin oranges and nuts along with the cherries or whatever fruit you're using as a garnish. Serve immediately or refrigerate.

ALL SOULS' DAY POMEGRANATE DESSERT

Serves 6–8

When my friends Joe and Gilda first offered me All Souls' Day pomegranates, I didn't know what to expect. This sticky conglomeration of kernels, seeds, and chunks looked like no other dessert I knew. And as soon as I tasted the crunchiness of the fruit and nuts in this sea of chocolate and honey I discovered something even more surprising: All Souls' Day Pomegranates are definitely habit-forming.

1. Place the cracked wheat in a pot. Pour in the 2 cups of cold water. Cover and let come to a rolling boil. Lower the heat. After 20 minutes, check to see if the water has been absorbed. If not, continue to cook the wheat until all the water is gone, checking every 5 minutes. Chill the wheat by spraying it with cold water; be sure to drain thoroughly.

2. While the wheat is cooking, slice the pomegranates in half. Peel and seed them, being sure not to leave on any pulp. Put the seeds into a large bowl.

3. When the wheat is cooked, cool and add it to the pomegranates.

4. Add the walnuts, chocolate slices and honey to the wheat and pomegranates. Mix well. Serve right away, or refrigerate for a few hours before serving.

1 cup hulled cracked wheat

2 cups cold water

5 cups pomegranate seeds (approximately 4 medium pomegranates)

2 cups walnuts, coarsely chopped

4 ounces milk chocolate (I use 20 Hershey's kisses), sliced in small pieces

8 ounces honey

BINTHA-CUSA

This recipe comes from Janice Corea Stack, who stopped by one day several Christmases ago to bring us the most beautiful sweet creation I had ever seen. A Bintha-Cusa is not the easiest dessert to make, but your time and effort will be rewarded with this elegant and delicious work of art that originated in the southwestern part of Italy called Calabria.

1. In a large bowl or mixer, sprinkle the yeast over the warm water, whisking it lightly to dissolve the yeast. If you are using fresh yeast, use a fork to mash the yeast thoroughly until it is dissolved in the water.

2. Add the sugar, salt, oil, cloves, cinnamon, and beaten eggs to the yeast and stir lightly.

3. Add the flour and shortening and mix well with a wooden spoon or your hands. Then add the wine to help the dough come together in a ball. If you are using a mixer with a dough hook, mix the flour in a cup at a time until the dough comes together.

4. Turn the dough out onto a well-floured surface (you'll need a good-sized area to work in, at least 3 feet square), sprinkle the ball of dough generously with flour, and knead continuously, sprinkling the dough with flour as you go along. Knead for 7 to 10 minutes, until the dough is soft and pliable and springs back when poked gently with your finger. It's important to knead the dough this long to mix the spices and other ingredients well and to prepare the dough for rolling.

5. Shape the dough into an oblong loaf and cover with a towel. Let rest for 15 minutes for dough to rise. Meanwhile, prepare the ingredients for the filling.

1. Prepare five pieces of brown paper (grocery bags will do) by cutting them into 12-inch squares and sprinkling them with flour. Place each piece of brown paper on a small cookie sheet or two on a large cookie sheet.

2. Punch the dough down, knead briefly, and form into a long loaf about the size of a meat loaf pan. Using a sharp knife, slice off five pieces that are 1/2 inch thick. Cover the remaining two thirds of the dough loaf with a towel and roll out each of the small dough pieces to a 10-inch circle. Place these individual "dishes," as they are called, on the five cookie sheets on top of the floured pieces of paper. Sprinkle each with a pinch of cinnamon

DOUGH

- 1 1/2 cups warm (not hot) tap water
- 2 ounces fresh yeast or 2 packages dry yeast, 1 ounce each
- 1/8 cup sugar
- 1 teaspoon salt
- 1/4 cup oil (preferably vegetable or 10 percent olive oil)
- 1/4 teaspoon ground cloves
- 1/2 teaspoon ground cinnamon
- 2 eggs, beaten
- 6 cups flour
- 1/3 cup vegetable shortening
- 1/4 cup Burgundy wine (or any other red wine)

FILLING

- 10 cups walnuts, coarsely chopped
- 10 cups raisins (plump by covering with warm water and letting stand for 15 minutes; drain before using)
- 2 1/2 teaspoons ground cloves
- 2 1/2 teaspoons ground cinnamon
- 2 1/2 cups oil, plus 3 1/4 cups oil

and cloves and smear each with two tablespoons of oil.

3. Divide the remaining loaf of dough into five equal pieces. Keeping the rest of the pieces of dough under a towel, roll out each one to a large circle 25 inches in diameter. The dough will be very thin, so you should keep your work surface well floured to avoid sticking.

4. When the dough is rolled out to the right size, sprinkle the surface with 1/2 teaspoon ground cloves and 1/2 teaspoon cinnamon, and rub the dough with the palm of your hand to make the dough colored.

5. Pour 1/2 cup oil onto the dough and rub evenly over the surface. Sprinkle evenly with 1/2 cup sugar, 2 cups of the walnuts, and 2 cups raisins.

6. Starting with the edge of the circle nearest you, fold over 2 inches of dough and cut along the far edge to separate the strip. Starting at one end, roll this strip into a snug roll (almost as if you were rolling a bandage) and place it upright in the middle of one of the "dishes" on the cookie sheets. It should resemble a rosette.

7. Fold over another 2 inches of dough and cut to make a second strip. Cut this second strip in two pieces, each 10 inches long, and roll each into a rosette. Place each rosette on the "dish," next to the center rosette.

8. Continue making rosettes from the dough until all the dough is used and the dish holds between 12 and 16 rosettes in two rings around the center rosette.

9. Pick up the overlapping dough of the "dish" and press it into the outside ring of rosettes. Loosely tie a string around the outside of the "dish" to hold the sides up during cooking.

10. Follow steps 9 through 14 for each of the remaining four pieces of dough.

11. Spoon 1 tablespoon of oil into and around each rosette, and bake the bintha-cusa at 375 degrees for 45 minutes. Then pour 2 tablespoons of honey over each rosette, and continue to bake for another 45 minutes. Remove from oven and pour 2 more tablespoons of honey over each rosette. Place on cooling rack and when completely cooled, wrap each Bintha-Cusa in foil. They will stay fresh for a week or longer, or they can be frozen.

VARIATION: Another method of rolling the Bintha-Cusa is to place a single rosette in the middle of each "dish" and then make a continuing spiral, working from the rosette out toward the edge of the dish.

2½ cups sugar
12½ cups honey

If you have any questions about the recipes, ingredients, or equipment used in this book, please don't hesitate to call us at Cremaldi's, 617-354-7969.

INDEX

beef soup with tortellini, 176
Grandma's Christmas Soup with
    Little Meat Balls, 174–75
spaghetti and meatballs, 99
stuffed red peppers, 221
tenderloin of beef stew with
    dumplings, 177
Tony Trio's Fancy Meat Ball, 204–5
veal and sausage cacciatore, 199
veal cutlets parmigiana, 202
veal fillets in lemon and caper sauce,
    199
veal pezzitine, 198
veal pocket, 196–97
veal roll in mustard cream, 200–1
Meat filling, 56
Meatless stuffed peppers, 222
Meat sauces
    Bolognese (ragù), 43, 73
    Grandmother's Three-Meat Tomato
        Sauce, 71
    Real Fast Meat Sauce, 43, 70
Mediterranean salad, 104
Milanese garlic soup, 158
Modenese filling, 57
Mozzarella cheese, 11–12
    buffalo mozzarella pizza, 122
    mozzarella di bufala insalata, 232
Mushrooms
    easy marinated mushrooms, 230
    stuffed mushrooms Italian style, 231
    See also Porcini
Mustard cream sauce, 200–201
My Father's Veal Pocket, 196–97
My Mother's Simple Chick-pea and
    Macaroni Soup, 167

Nutmeg macaroni, 34, 43
Nuts
    anchovy-pine nut-currant sauce, 43,
        44, 83
    basil-pine nut sausage, 146
    fruit and nut filling, 62–63
    spinach-nut sauce, 43, 44, 75

Oil, 10
Olive (Gaeta) sauce, 43, 44, 72
Onions

risotto with porcini and onions, 98–
    99
sweet onion pizza, 118
Oranges
    orange macaroni, 36, 43
    orange-ricotta gnocchi, 41, 44
    orange sauce, 43, 44, 68, 85
    orange-spice sausage, 149

Panini ("little breads"), 112–13
Parmesan cheese, 11
    basil-Parmesan butter, zucchini soup
        with, 172–73
Parmigiana pizza, 123
Parsley, 13
    parsley filling, 58
    parsley macaroni, 34, 43
    parsley sauce, 43, 68, 74
Pasta. See Macaroni headings
Pasta machines, 22
Pea soup, 169
Penne with prosciutto, baked, 94
Pepper, black, 12
    black pepper macaroni, 31, 44
Peppercorns, pink, 12–13
    pink peppercorn macaroni, 31, 43
    shrimp with pink peppercorn sauce,
        189
Pepperoni
    chicken breasts with pepperoni
        mousse, 210–11
    pepperoni and chicken sausage, 146–
        47
Peppers, green
    meatless stuffed peppers, 222
    three-pepper pizza, 121
Peppers, red
    artichoke and vinegared peppers
        pizza, 125
    red pepper macaroni, 32, 44
    roasted red peppers, anchovy, and
        garlic, 155
    stuffed red peppers, 221
    summer squash and red pepper
        soup, 172
    three-pepper pizza, 121
Pesto
    cheese tortellini salad in pesto, 103